True Crime Stories

12 Shocking True
Crime Murder Cases

True Crime Anthology Vol.1

By
Jack Rosewood

Free Bonus!

Contents

Introduction

In the annals of criminal history, most cases are open and shut. A crime takes place, the police investigate, an arrest is made, and the accused is either acquitted or convicted of said crime. Some criminal cases make for interesting prime time specials or cable network documentaries, but few invoke mysteries that persist for any length of time.

But some crimes are so puzzling and perplexing that the mystery surrounding them takes on a life of its own. It is these mysterious crimes that often have the greatest impact on all involved.

Crime in general has profound effects on the victims specifically and the greater society in general. Murders, in particular, leave behind gaping psychological wounds that often only begin to heal when the perpetrator is caught and convicted for his/her crimes.

But what happens when the murderer is never identified? Or worse yet, what happens when the victim is never found, as if the person vanished into thin air?

These are the type of crimes that tear at the social fabric of a community more than any other – crimes where a suspect is never identified, a body is never found, or a reason for the crime is never determined.

The world is full of many mysteries and within the pages of this book you will be introduced to twelve of the most intriguing and amazing mysteries in modern criminal history. Some of the cases here involve multiple crimes where coincidences seem to link what are otherwise unrelated cases. Investigation of these cases reveals that sometimes although events may be creepy, they are in fact coincidences; while in other cases the jury is still out.

A number of high-profile disappearances are also given consideration in the following pages. While a mysterious fog of uncertainty still hangs over one of these cases, excellent police work and modern science helped locate other missing individuals.

Finally, this e-book considers a number of unsolved murder cases that were all but forgotten about and went "cold," only to heat up and get resolved years, even decades, later through advances in science and new eyewitness testimony.

The world is truly and amazing place full of many mysteries, which includes the criminal world as you will see in this intriguing and exciting e-book.

CHAPTER 1:
A Killer Coincidence?
The Mary Morris Murders

In the 1984 science fiction classic *The Terminator*, a murderous cyborg from the future played by Arnold Schwarzenegger, hunted women in Los Angeles named Sarah Connor in order to stop a woman with that same name from giving birth to a man who would kill the cyborg's masters in the future. The plot was totally outlandish and not meant to portray or emulate any real event or situation, but a pair of murders in Houston, Texas in 2000 shocked area residents and to sci-fi fans it appeared to be a case of reality imitating art.

In the span of less than one week, two women both named Mary Morris were murdered in eerily similar ways in Houston. Once the local media made the connections between the two women's names, then other connections were quickly made: the two women looked alike, the manner of their murders was similar, and their bodies were discovered in similar locations. With that many similarities most people were convinced that the murders were somehow connected.

Was a serial killer using the *Terminator* as an inspiration for his sick homicidal fantasies?

The residents of Houston were on edge in the late months of 2000. Anyone could be the killer, and any woman named Mary Morris could be the next victim!

Mary Henderson Morris

Mary Henderson Morris was a forty-eight-year-old wife and mother who worked hard as a loan officer at Chase Bank in Houston. She and her husband had built a good life for themselves and lived in the reasonably affluent Houston neighborhood of Spring Valley. They were hardworking, successful people who were well liked by the neighbors, friends, and family. By all accounts, the couple had a good relationship and neither was involved in drugs or criminal activity, which makes this part of the case the most puzzling.

The morning of October 12, 2000, began as any other in the Morris household. Mary woke up first, got ready for work, and left the house about six am. But Mary never made it to work.

Mary's husband of five years, Jay, usually spoke with her several times during the day on the phone, so he began to worry when the afternoon came and he had yet to hear from his wife. Mary's daughter from a previous marriage, Marilyn Blalock, and Jay filed a missing person report early that evening about the same time a burned car was discovered in a vacant field.

A call was made to the Harris County Sheriff's Department at about 10 am that morning about what was believed to be burning debris or leaves. Later in the day, police arrived at the wooded area to find that it was not debris or leaves that were burning, but an automobile. After the fire was put out the sheriff's department determined that a charred female body was inside. It was the body of Mary Henderson Morris.

The fire made it impossible for coroners to determine the method of death, although it was quickly ruled a homicide. A search revealed that Morris' purse and wedding ring were missing, which suggested robbery, but too many questions remained.

If it were a robbery, why was her car not taken? Why would a robber, or robbers, go to such lengths to conceal part of their crime?

The crime was obviously not a carjacking because the car was burned. Even if it were an attempted carjacking gone bad, there would have been no reason to take the car and its owner to a remote location, kill the owner, and then burn the car.

And why was the car dumped and burned in a vacant lot?

The more investigators looked at the case, the less it made sense.

There were also no witnesses to her abduction or murder.

Due to the circumstances, authorities quickly determined that this was no ordinary murder case, but little did they know how extraordinary the case would become.

Just four days later, after the Morris family put Mary to rest on October 16, Blaylock made the painful, yet seemingly simple journey to the coroner's office to retrieve some of her mother's personal effects.

Instead she walked into an episode from the *Twilight Zone*.

"They told me they still had Mary Morris' body," recalled Blaylock. "I was freaking out. I was thinking we just had the funeral. I saw the remains, and I was looking at something that wasn't even my mother."

It turns out that the woman Marilyn Blaylock saw on the coroner's table was not her mother, but was in fact another woman named Mary Morris—Mary McGinnis Morris!

Mary McGinnis Morris

In many ways other than just the name, Mary McGinnis Morris shared a number of similarities with Mary Henderson Morris, which makes this case all that more eerie. Although Mary McGinnis was a bit younger than Mary Henderson at thirty-nine years old, both women were attractive, gregarious brunettes. Mary McGinnis was also a professional woman who shared a nice suburban home with her husband.

On October 16, 2000, the Harris County Sheriff's Department found the body of Mary McGinnis Morris badly beaten with a single gunshot to her head in a location about twenty-five miles from where Mary Henderson Morris was found days earlier.

Mary McGinnis was also found murdered in her car in a vacant lot in Harris County. Although the vacant lots were located on different ends of the county, both spots had an eerie familiarity.

In life and death, the two women shared some uncanny similarities, which raised the obvious question—who would want to kill the two Marys?

Suspects and Theories

Although authorities were at a loss trying to find suspects and reasons for the murder of Mary Henderson Morris, they quickly zeroed in on two potential perps for the Mary McGinnis case.

At the time of her death, Mary McGinnis worked as a nurse practitioner and medical director at Union Carbide in Houston. Her supervisors noted that she was a good employee who got along with all of her co-workers and likewise almost all of her co-workers liked Mary, with the exception of one—Duane Young.

Duane Young was a nurse who worked alongside Mary, and as their time working together progressed, he apparently became obsessed with her. Young's obsession with Mary began innocently enough; he hung around her desk at work and engaged her in conversation whenever he could. The behavior at first seemed to Mary McGinnis to be more of a "puppy love" type situation than that of an obsessed maniac, but eventually Young's façade of a "lost puppy dog" was lifted to reveal the stalker that he was. As Young's menacing looks and comments towards Mary reached a creepy crescendo, she found the words "death to her" scrawled on her desk calendar. After numerous complaints to her bosses about Young's inappropriate and borderline illegal behavior, which was verified by co-workers, the stalker nurse was fired on October 13, just two days before Mary disappeared. The note scrawled on Mary's desk proved to be the last straw.

Weeks before her disappearance and death, Mary McGinnis bought a handgun that she kept hidden in her car. Owning a gun in the United States, especially in the state of Texas, is no big deal, and some even consider it not just a right, but an obligation. Mary McGinnis, though, was never a hunter or gun enthusiast, so when she started packing a pistol, her closest friends and family members knew that she was frightened of something or someone. Although Mary was a bit of a private person, she apparently felt that the threats from Young, or perhaps someone else, were grave enough that she needed to be armed because she did tell a couple of her closest friends about the handgun. Mary was no expert in firearms, so her husband gave her the gun and showed her how to use it.

Also, the day Young was fired Mary's employers told her to stay home in order to defuse the situation, which turned into a scene anyway, as Young demanded to see Mary and had to be escorted out of the premises.

October 15th was the last day Mary was seen alive.

By all accounts it was another Sunday for Mary McGinnis; she ran a number of errands and visited a friend named Laurie Gemmell. According to Gemmell, McGinnis called her from a store during the afternoon to tell her, "There is someone here who is giving me the creeps." Not long after that call, McGinnis then called 911.

The transcript of the 911 call has never been released to the public, but a detective who worked on the case and heard the tape said that it, "had their blood chilled listening to it."

After the 911 call, Mary McGinnis' trail went cold.

When Mary did not return home that evening, her husband of seventeen years, Mike, filled a missing person report. In an unfortunate twist that brought Mary McGinnis' case together with Mary Henderson's, the body of McGinnis was found shot to death in a vacant lot outside of Houston.

Despite the similarities of both women being found murdered in their cars, the method of murder was clear in the McGinnis case—she had died of a single gunshot to the head from her own gun.

At first glance, it looked like a suicide, but as homicide investigators examined the scene more closely, they learned that the scene looked staged and it was instead a poor attempt to throw them off. Mary had been beaten and gagged, and her car keys were left outside the car.

Investigators quickly learned about Duane Young, who then went to the top of their suspect list. But as homicide detectives looked into Young's background, Mike Morris soon joined Young as a person of interest.

Morris supplied investigators with samples of his DNA and gave initial interviews, but he declined to take a polygraph exam, hired an attorney, and refused to cooperate with investigators as the case dragged on. Morris also refused to allow his sixteen year old daughter to be interviewed by police. Since it is a person's constitutional right not to talk to police in the United States, Morris did nothing legally wrong in that respect, although his actions placed him further under the police radar.

The more investigators focused on Morris, the more they learned that there was trouble in paradise at the Morris household. Although it was never proved, allegations of infidelity by both Mike and Mary surfaced. Infidelity is always considered as a motive in spousal murder. Whether it is murder to get rid of a spouse in order to be with a paramour, or done out of anger towards a cheating spouse, unfaithfulness must always be considered motive by police. The infidelity motive seemed to go nowhere but it was not long before more perplexing inconsistencies came to light.

It was learned that Mike had taken out a $500,000 life insurance policy on Mary, which alone is not enough to convict or even get someone arrested for murder, but greed is one of the most common motivations for murder throughout history.

Then there was the mysterious phone call.

Records indicate that on the afternoon of October 15th, about two hours after she called 911, Mary received a call on her cell phone from Mike. Mike claims that he did in fact make the call when he was with his daughter at a movie, but that the call went straight to voice mail. Records show that the call was answered and lasted for four minutes. Morris claimed that the phone company must have made a mistake! Although it is possible that the phone company could have made a mistake, it seemed extremely convenient for the suspect in a murder investigation that such a mistake, which is nearly unheard of, would happen at this critical juncture.

Mary McGinnis was also not robbed. In fact, the only valuable item that appeared to have been taken from her was a ring, which was later found in the possession of their daughter. Mike later told investigators that his wife had lost the ring before her murder and that he and his daughter had found it in the house later.

The final piece of circumstantial evidence that points towards Mike Morris as the perpetrator in his wife's murder is the actual murder weapon. The gun that was used to kill Mary McGinnis was actually Mike's gun. He gave the gun to Mary after Duane Young's stalking reached its peak, and only he and some of Mary's closest friends even knew about the gun or where she hid it underneath the seat.

Clearly, many of Mary's friends, law enforcement, and the people of Houston in general began to think Mike was good for his wife's murder, but the evidence was just not there to make an arrest, never mind win a conviction in front of a jury.

Eventually, Mike and his daughter moved back to his native West Virginia where he still presumably lives to this day.

But even if Mike Morris or Duane Young was responsible for the murder of Mary McGinnis Morris, the elephant in the room remains: was her murder connected to Mary Henderson Morris'?

A Hit Gone Wrong?

Once the theory of a homicidal cyborg from the future that came to Houston to kill women named Mary Morris was eliminated, investigators were left trying to determine if the two crimes were connected or just some strange, macabre coincidence. It is difficult to get past the two victims similar names, appearance, the type of location where the bodies were discovered, the manner in which they were killed.

Because of the plethora of similarities, many have concluded that either Mike Morris or Duane Young hired a hitman to kill Mary McGinnis, but in a cruel case of mistaken identity also killed Mary Henderson.

An anonymous caller to the *Houston Chronicle* said: "They got the wrong Mary Morris," in reference to the murder of Mary Henderson Morris.

But investigators remain unconvinced that the two homicides are related.

"As far as the dates go, they are so close they could be linked," said Harris County sheriff's detective Wayne Kuhlman. "But when someone is hired to kill someone, they are going to have their information and know their habits. Hit men don't just go out with nothing."

As of 2016 both cases remain cold.

Sometimes reality is stranger than fiction.

CHAPTER 2:

The Disappearances of the Palmer Brothers

It seems that in the world today one is never far from another person. In the decades just before World War II, the most industrialized nations witnessed a rapid migration of their populations from rural to urban and suburban areas. Because of that trend, most of us have to travel a distance to truly get away from the noise of civilization. Even denizens of rural areas are usually not very far from their closest neighbors and only a short drive to the nearest town or city. In areas that are more remote, such as the American west, freeways, trains, and airplanes connect formerly isolated areas to the rest of the world.

The American state of Alaska may be an exception to this rule.

Alaska, the United States' forty-ninth state, is aptly named the "Last Frontier" because of its vast expanses of territory that has rarely, if ever, been walked on by human feet. The size of Alaska is immense; it is comprised of 663,268 square miles of land, which makes it by far the largest American state and larger than all but twenty of the independent nation-states of the world.

In contrast to Alaska's vast size, its population is relatively modest. With only 710,231 inhabitants, Alaska ranks forty seventh out of fifty American states in population and nearly half of those reside in the Anchorage metropolitan area.

Alaska's vastness has become somewhat of a pop culture phenomenon in recent years, with a number of television shows being produced there, such as *Tougher in Alaska*, that chronicle the harshness of the Alaska frontier. The book and movie *Into the Wild*, based on the true life adventures of Christopher McCandless, also depicted the beauty and range of the Alaskan frontier while also showing its potentially dangerous side.

If there is anywhere in the industrialized world where one can get lost, it is Alaska!

In fact, in the United States, Alaska has the dubious distinction of having the most missing persons per capita, more than twice the national average.

People disappear into the Alaskan wilderness every year and some, such as Christopher McCandless, even do so willingly, which at first glance makes the next case seem like just another missing person file from Alaska; but further examination of the Palmer brothers' disappearances reveals another set of bizarre coincidences that are stranger than fiction.

A Family of Men

The Palmer family seemed to be made for life in Alaska. A family of men, the siblings included oldest brother Chris, middle brother Charles "Chuckie", youngest brother Michael, and sister Hannah. The three boys and their sister grew up together in Wasilla, Alaska, which has become famous in recent years for being the home of former Alaska governor and vice presidential candidate, Sarah Palin. The three Palmer brothers enjoyed spending time with each other and engaging in typical Alaskan activities including hiking, fishing, hunting, and snowmobiling. They enjoyed the rugged frontier lifestyle of Alaska and all it has to offer.

Life in Alaska was good for the Palmer family, until things took a bizarre and tragic turn on June 3, 1999.

The Disappearance of Michael

Fifteen-year-old Michael Palmer was enjoying his summer vacation from school the same way many American boys his age do—hanging out with his friends and pushing the boundaries of his parents and the law. On that night, he slept over at a friend's house, and after his friend's parents went to bed the crew snuck out of the house to see what kind of trouble they could get into.

Michael and his friends went to a few different parties that night and engaged in some drinking, although his friends would later say that none of them, including Michael, were too drunk to navigate their bicycles. The group spent their time at the parties drinking some beer, visiting with friends who they had not seen since the end of the school year, and trying to make time with girls. At one party, a fight broke out that Michael was involved in, but he was not believed to be the reason for the fight, and like everything else during the night, it was not considered out of the ordinary—just some tough Alaska boys blowing off some steam.

After a couple hours of party hopping, the boys decided to ride their bikes back to the home of the boy they were supposed to be staying the night with. Although the nine-mile ride was fairly long, Michael and his friends were all in good shape and used to such long treks across the vast Alaskan outdoors. The boys rode in single file with Michael taking up the rear, but when they arrived at the house, Michael was nowhere to be seen.

Michael Palmer had vanished into thin air!

The boys later told authorities that they thought Michael had changed his mind and decided to ride home to sleep in his own bed, so they did not report him missing until later the next day. Once Michael was reported missing, the local authorities and the Palmer family began their search in earnest.

Local police quickly found Michael's bike in a river, but were quick to state that they did not believe he drowned. The boy was athletic and knew how to swim, the river was fairly shallow, and a log jam down river would have caught his body if he did in fact drown.

The next major clue was even more puzzling. Michael's shoes were found wet and neatly placed side-by-side next to an airstrip about 200 yards from the river. No airplane had taken off the night of the boy's disappearance and the neat placement of the shoes suggests that Michael placed them there. They were not strewn about as if there had been a struggle.

But some started to believe that Michael was the victim of violence that began at one of the parties he attended on June 3. The police interviewed and gave polygraph examinations to everyone who was known to have been at the parties, with special attention given to boys involved in the fight that was mentioned earlier. Everyone passed their polygraph exams.

It should be noted that people often "beat" polygraph exams, but those who do are usually adults who are often seasoned criminals, not high school boys who got into a fist fight.

Besides, how many teenagers can keep a secret? It seems that if one of Michael's classmates had something to do with his disappearance then someone would have said something by now.

But the disappearance of Michael Palmer quickly grew as cold as an Alaskan winter.

The Disappearance of Chucky Palmer

Perhaps the worst part of losing a loved one to a disappearance is the unknown. For years the Palmer family wondered what had happened to Michael. Was he abducted and murdered? Did he become disorientated and wander deep into the forest where he died? The disappearance of Michael Palmer faded from the memory of the people of Wasilla but was never totally forgotten. Conspiracy theories based on no credible evidence began to circulate, and before too long Michael's disappearance became legendary in that part of Alaska. But to the Palmer family, the loss of their youngest brother was never legendary; it was the source of constant pain and a void that could not be filled.

As the years passed by, the other Palmer children became adults and started families of their own. They never forgot about Michael, but the pain of losing him diminished somewhat, and the family finally looked to be moving on. The siblings remained close in adulthood, especially brothers

Charles "Chucky" Jr. and Chris, taking part in many typical Alaskan adventures in the outdoors.

But the thought of what happened to their youngest brother was never far from their minds.

"Two brothers aren't supposed to go missing from the same family," is what oldest brother Chris said when the seemingly impossible happened – his brother Chucky vanished into thin air in much the same circumstances as Michael.

On April 10, 2010, nearly eleven years after Michael disappeared, Chucky, Chris, and some of their friends went on a snowmobile trip on Bald Mountain, about an hour outside of Wasilla. April in Alaska is still cold enough to support winter sports; but spring is usually right around the corner, so the most hardcore Alaskans often like to get one last skiing, snowmobiling, or ice fishing trip in during that month.

In the morning, it seemed to the Palmer brothers that they had picked a good day for their end of the season snowmobile trip. The weather was nice, and there was plenty of snow left on the mountain for the men to make plenty of trails, but before the men even got started, signs pointed towards an impending tragedy. Oldest brother Chris, who was a much more experience snowmobiler than Chucky, had to stay behind because the handlebars on his snowmobile snapped. Not wanting to miss out on possibly the last chance of the season to snowmobile, Chucky continued on with his friends. Interestingly though, Chucky, who was admittedly the weakest snowmobiler in the group, brought up the rear of the convoy much like his brother Michael did with his friends eleven years earlier.

Unfortunately for the Palmer family the result was the same!

Chucky, like Michael, disappeared into thin air. As soon as Chucky's friends noticed that the thirty-one-year-old was missing, they retraced their tracks and searched Bald Mountain for their friend. As minutes turned into hours, the situation became more desperate, and professional search teams from Alaska Mountain Rescue were called in to find the missing Palmer brother. Snow and low visibility hampered the search teams, but once the snow stopped searchers located Chucky's snowmobile.

Chucky's snowmobile was found off the main path in a drift with no footprints nearby. Many people think that the lack of footprints is the most eerie aspect of the case, but there is no reason why there would be any since Bald Mountain was the recipient of over two feet of snow at the time.

The search continued after the snow melted, but no body or further clues were ever discovered on Bald Mountain. It was as if the mountain just swallowed Chucky whole.

With Chucky's mountain disappearance, the remaining Palmer family and the entire world for that matter, is left wondering how this is possible and what are the chances? Even if foul play were responsible for the disappearance of one or both of the Palmer brothers, the chances of that happening twice in the same family must be extremely small. Most people could never imagine such a thing happening once in their family, never mind twice.

Perhaps Chris Palmer best summoned up his family's tragedies in layman's terms: "I never thought I'd have to deal with this shit ever again."

The world will probably never know what happened to the Palmer brothers, but they are proof that lightning can strike twice!

CHAPTER 3:
The Liquid Matthew Case

Some of you reading this may have been to a dinner party theater production, which have become popular over the last several years. If you have not been to one of these productions, the concept is interesting: as the diners enjoy a meal, a play takes place that usually involves some type of murder mystery. The audience/diners are often encouraged to get involved by offering their clues and/or theories concerning the crime.

In the end, the caper is solved, the cast takes a bow, and everyone goes home full and satisfied with an interesting night out.

Several of you have also probably taken part in a scavenger hunt at some point in your lives. Some of the most elaborate scavenger hunts take place over several miles of territory and sometimes, like dinner party theater, involve a fictional crime that has taken place. In order to solve the fictional crime you have to locate a clue, which then leads you to the next clue in another part of town and so on and so forth. The clues are often written as cryptic poems that, to those not involved in the game, would seem very bizarre and creepy.

For those of you who have been a part of a dinner party theater or a crime based scavenger hunt, you probably have fond memories of the event.

But what if your scavenger hunt somehow miraculously became part of a real murder investigation?

That is exactly what happened in suburban Miami on December 6, 1983. The case became known as the "Liquid Matthew Case" because of cryptic writings that were found at the scene of an apparent homicide.

A Body and Cryptic Clues

On the morning of December 6, 1983, residents of the quiet Miami suburb of Hialeah, Florida awoke to the grim display of what appeared to be a corpse on the side of a road. Local police were quickly called to scene and after searching the body, determined that the male had fallen victim to murder. The body showed signs of strangulation, but little more than that could be determined. The victim had no identification on him, and area residents did not know who the man was. At first, the police could only say that the man was a Hispanic John Doe.

Homicide detectives cordoned off the area and began their search for the usual forensic evidence—a murder weapon, footprints, or even a blood trail.

But the evidence they found proved to be truly unsettling, even for veteran detectives.

Taped to a nearby sign, investigators noticed a bag, and within that bag was a handwritten note that said, "Now the motive is clear and the victim is too. You've got all the answers. Just follow the clues."

At first, the investigators believed the note was some type of prank. What else would explain the cryptic note being found at the scene? After all, only in *Batman* movies do criminals leave riddles at the scene for law enforcement to solve. In fact, some police officers on the scene thought that it may be the work of some sort of scavenger hunt, although that would not explain the dead body laying just feet away. But when they found another note taped to the back of a nearby speed limit sign, they began to fear a psychotic killer was on the loose in suburban Miami.

"Yes, Matthew is dead, but his body not felt. Those brains were not Matt's because his body did melt. For Billy threw Matthew in some hot boiling oil. To confuse the police for the mystery they did toil," read the contents of the second note.

The police were confused and confounded with the cryptic message. What did it mean? Was Matthew the name of the Hispanic John Doe? Was a man named Billy his killer?

As the authorities struggled to find answers in the bizarre murder mystery, which became known as the "Liquid Matthew Case," the public became extremely frightened when the details emerged. The residents of sleepy Hialeah were just as confused as the police and afraid that a thrill killer or serial killer was operating on their streets.

Residents of the community began to barricade their homes and arm themselves for a potential showdown with a serial killer, and the local police began working overtime to solve the enigmatic crime.

But the investigation soon turned up a benign explanation for the notes.

The Explanation

As the police investigation into the Liquid Matthew Case progressed and its details were made public, it was learned that the notes were actually part of a Halloween murder mystery game/scavenger hunt sponsored by four area churches. It turns out that the notes and the game fell victim to the rainy south Florida climate. After the game was completed, organizers failed to pick up all of the notes because heavy rains that swamped the Miami area.

As for the victim?

Police eventually identified "Liquid Matthew" as a Columbian sailor named Francisco Patino Gutierrez. It is believed that Gutierrez was probably killed in one of the many drug smuggling schemes that were prevalent in Miami during the 1980s, but the details remain unknown.

With that said, local authorities can say unequivocally that Gutierrez's murder and the cryptic scavenger hunt notes were not connected in any way. He was not boiled to death and whatever his killer, or killers, name was, it was clear that the person had no intention of even remotely identifying himself.

The Liquid Matthew Case was just one big bizarre coincidence.

CHAPTER 4:
The Brighton Trunk Murders

The "Queen of Watering Places"

The city of Brighton, United Kingdom, often known colloquially as "Brighton Beach", has been one of the prime destinations for the British for over 200 years. Brighton boasts of some of the nicest beaches in Britain, relatively warmer temperatures compared to the rest of the country, and a plethora of bars, nightclubs and concert venues. Because of these things, Brighton has earned the nickname the "Queen of Watering Places."

Besides being a top vacation destination, Brighton has also been known as a safe, peaceful city. Outside of a spate of counter-culture youth violence during the 1960s and '70s—which was made known to the world through the rock band The Who's 1973 album *Quadrophenia* and a 1979 film of the same name, as well as the popular Stray Cat's song "Rumble in Brighton"—and the Irish Republican Army bombing of a hotel in 1984, crime in Brighton has been historically low.

Therefore, Brighton's idyllic setting makes this next case, or series of cases, especially interesting.

During the course of just over 100 years, Brighton was the scene of three bizarre, similar yet unrelated murders. Another murder that took place in London shared many of the hallmarks of the other three murders and was also determined to be unrelated. Collectively, these four murders are known as the "Brighton Trunk Murders."

Due to their mysterious and bizarre circumstances, any one of the trunk murders could probably be given its own entry in this anthology. When considered as a group, due to the coincidence factor, the Brighton Trunk Murders are probably the strangest case examined in this book.

The 1831 Murder

In 1831, Brighton was in the middle of one of its early boom periods. Tea, spices, and gold were flowing into England from its lucrative colonies in India and South Africa, which resulted in a trickle-down effect of wealth whereby the middle class was growing at a phenomenal rate. The result was good for Brighton, as members of the growing middle class were able to travel to the beachfront community on new rail lines and spend their disposable income in the city's bars and shops. Life was good in Brighton, and most of its inhabitants were happy.

Celia Holloway was an exceptional woman for her time; she was a painter on the chain pier who was not reliant on her husband John. She spent her days painting the ocean, beaches, and anyone who passed by. Celia was a happy, independent woman who lived in a time when it was not common for women to have those views or lifestyle. The progressive-minded Brighton seemed to be the perfect place for her to pursue her interests while she was happily married to John.

But sometimes things are not as they seem.

Apparently, John was not happy being married to a liberated woman, so he murdered her, placed her body in a trunk, and then buried the trunk under Lover's Walk. John Holloway was quickly arrested for his wife's murder, convicted, and hanged all within a year. Justice was quick in nineteenth century Britain.

So began the long, bizarre saga of the Brighton Trunk Murders.

Minnie Bonati

Although the next murder in the series of Brighton Trunk Murders took place in London, which is about fifty miles from the sea resort city, the circumstances of the crime are eerily similar enough to the others that it warrants being included in this macabre list. On May 7, 1927, an attendant at the Charing Cross train station in London became concerned with a foul smell emanating from the luggage room. Upon investigating the odor, he soon learned that source was a luggage trunk. Correctly believing that he may have stumbled onto a crime, the local police were called to investigate.

The police discovered a grisly scene—a dismembered body with each piece wrapped in paper. Also included in the trunk were several items of clothing, including a pair of underwear marked "P. Holt."

The circumstances of the discovery shocked and frightened Londoners when it became public. The average Londoner at the time was a street-smart person and no stranger to crime. Theft, prostitution, and even murder were all crimes that Londoners were used to hearing about in 1927, but this was quite different. Most of the murders that took place in London at the time were cases of criminals preying on each other, personal and/or financial grudges, or of someone ending up in the wrong part of town. Murders with this level of brutality were almost unheard—almost.

It was less than fifty years earlier, in 1888, when five women were raped and murdered in London's east end in the "Jack the Ripper" murders. In 1927, when the dismembered body was found in the train station, some of the older residents of London were reminded of the Jack the Ripper case and wondered if there might be some connection.

But the London Police quickly dismissed any such outlandish claims as they quietly pieced together the identity of the victim.

After a thorough investigation, police learned that the woman to whom the underwear belonged was still alive, but that one of her former employees, thirty-six-year-old Minnie Rolls/Bonati, could not be located. Fearing that the case would go cold, investigators went public with the details and soon a taxi driver came forward who said that he gave a ride to a man with a large trunk in tow to the Charing Cross station on May 6.

Police eventually identified the man as thirty-six-year-old real estate agent John Robinson. Under pressure during police questioning, Robinson eventually admitted to the murder and dismemberment stating: "I met her at Victoria and took her to my office. I want to tell you all about it. I done it and cut her up." Robinson claimed self-defense to the police. He said that after he brought Bonati back to his office, for some reason she attacked him, so he defended himself with a coal shovel, hitting her in the head with a fatal blow. He then dismembered her body in the office, placed it in a trunk, and called for a taxi to take him to the train station.

Perhaps he believed that since Bonati was a prostitute no one would care and he could get away with the murder, but the dismemberment was much too much for the civilized nature of early twentieth century London.

The mountain of physical evidence, along with his confession, was too much for Robinson to overcome in trial. He was quickly convicted and executed on August 12, 1927, just over two months after the murder.

The "Girl with the Pretty Feet"

By 1934, the luster of Brighton beach had worn off a bit as the United Kingdom, along with most of the industrialized world, was in the midst of the Great Depression. The crowds that had flocked to Brighton's beaches dwindled as the average British citizen found saving what little money he had more important than a weekend at the beach. To most people at the time, the Great Depression seemed to have made Brighton's golden age a thing of the distant past, which was further exacerbated by a series of macabre events that began in June of that year.

On June 17, an unclaimed trunk at Brighton train station was noticed by an employee. The employee, William Vinnicombe, was not alarmed so much by the trunk being left at the station, but more so by the foul odor coming from it. Perhaps aware of the 1927 murder of Minnie Bonati, Vinnicombe called local police to investigate the trunk's contents.

Chief inspector Ronald Donaldson quickly learned that like the Bonati case, he was staring at the dismembered corpse of a woman!

In fact, the trunk only contained the woman's torso, head, and arms; the legs were recovered in a suitcase the next day at another train station.

Unlike the Bonati case, there were few clues to the dead woman's identity tucked into the trunk. A piece of paper with the word, or name, "Ford" was found in the trunk, but it was never determined if it was connected to victim, if it was a "red herring", or possibly some random paper that ended up in the trunk. A coroner's examination determined that the woman was around twenty-five years old and pregnant. A cause of death was never determined. The manner of death could have been an accident, but the brutal dismemberment of the body clearly pointed towards homicide. The Jane Doe quickly became known as "the girl with the pretty feet" because her feet were believed to be those of a dancer's.

But someone would notice if a dancer was missing—at least that is what investigators believed. Unfortunately for the girl with the pretty feet, no one came forward on her behalf, which led many to believe that the victim was a prostitute.

Going on the prostitute theory, investigators scoured brothels and red light districts and began to focus on a family doctor who often performed illegal abortions on the side, often for prostitutes. The suspect was a man named Edward Massiah, who lived in the neighboring town of Hove.

Although Donaldson suspected Massiah, the medical examiner who performed Jane Doe's autopsy was not so sure, as he noted that the dismemberment did not appear to be the work of a professional.

Massiah was also apparently well connected with local police and politicians.

Donaldson's superiors forced him to back off of his investigation of Massiah, who then quietly moved to London where he continued to practice medicine, both legally and illegally. Any doubts concerning Massiah's influential connections were put to rest when a woman whom he performed an abortion on died, but he was never charged.

Massiah retired to the Caribbean in the 1950s and the case of the girl with the pretty feet was never solved.

As strange as the case of the girl with the pretty feet was, it was made even stranger when it was revealed that another trunk murder case was taking place in Brighton at the same time!

The Murder of Violette Kay/Saunders

Forty-two-year-old Violette Kay and Minnie Bonati shared some dubious distinctions—they were both prostitutes who were both murdered, dismembered, and then shoved into a trunk. It is doubtful if either Kay or Bonati ever saw herself working as a prostitute and there is no possible way that either

35

could have foreseen the awful circumstances in which their lives ended.

Violette Kaye, also known as Violette Saunders, worked as a prostitute in the Brighton area and dated a twenty-six-year-old man known as Toni Mancini, although his legal name was Cecil England. For legitimate work, Mancini worked as a bartender and bouncer at local bars, but his true passion was in the world of crime. He was known to the local police as a low level player in the local criminal underworld—a thug who the heavier players could employ to do dirty work.

Although Mancini worked as a bouncer and occasional heavy for underworld figures, the majority of his violence was reserved for those closest to him. He was known to slap his girlfriends around in front of others if they did not do as he pleased, but Violette Kaye was a bit different than his other girlfriends. Kaye was known to stand up to Mancini's threats and violence and would even fight back.

Kaye and Mancini's relationship was volatile to say the least.

The fact that Kaye was nearly twenty years older than her paramour contributed to the turbulent nature of their relationship, as she was lacking in self-esteem and jealous to the point of violence. Kaye and Mancini frequently drank copious amounts of alcohol, which then turned their drinking sessions into shouting matches and sometimes fisticuffs. It was during one of these drinking sessions that Violette Kaye was seen alive for the last time.

On the night of May 10, Kaye and Mancini were drinking heavily at Mancini's place of employment, the Skylark Café. As the drinking binge progressed, Kaye accused Mancini of having an affair with a young female employee at the bar named Elizabeth Attrell. Questions by Kaye turned into loud accusations as she began to become more intoxicated, and before she and Mancini left for the evening, the two were witnessed shoving each other.

That was the last time anyone saw Violette Kaye alive.

In the days after May 10, Mancini acted extremely suspicious, giving some of Kaye's personal effects to Attrell and telling Violette's friends and family that she had suddenly moved to Paris. Kaye's sister then received a telegram that claimed to be from her sister in Paris, but it was later revealed that the message was in fact sent from Brighton.

Mancini then took up residence in an apartment near the Brighton train station, in the days after the dismembered body of the girl with the pretty feet was discovered.

As the local police searched the area around the train station for clues to murder of the Jane Doe, they eventually conducted a house to house search, which led them to the apartment of

Toni Mancini. Once inside Mancini's apartment, they were quickly overwhelmed with the smell of decay.

They found the body of Violette Kaye stuffed into a trunk at the foot of Mancini's bed!

The public was surprised at the eerie turn of events. How could there be two extremely brutal, yet similar, murders committed at the same time in the quiet vacation resort town of Brighton?

Certainly Toni Mancini must be the killer of both women, right?

The police quickly determined that Mancini was not the perpetrator of the Jane Doe murder; it was just simply another bizarre coincidence in the series of "trunk murders" as they became known. They were confident, however, that Mancini killed Kaye in act of anger on the night of May 10. An autopsy, which was conducted by the same doctor who examined the remains of the girl with the pretty feet, concluded that Kaye died from a blow to the head.

Mancini went to trial for Kaye's murder in late 1934, which the prosecution believed would be an open and shut case. The fact that Kaye's rotting corpse was discovered in Mancini's apartment was thought to be damning evidence alone, but for good measure the prosecution paraded a litany of witnesses who all testified to the defendant's seedy nature. Former and current girlfriends, one who testified that Mancini tried to get her to give him a false alibi to the police, and criminal associates all gave proof, in the prosecution's eyes, that Mancini was the type of person who would murder his girlfriend.

But the strategy backfired.

The defense acknowledged that their client had a criminal background, which is why he attempted to hide Kaye's body *after* he found her dead. The defense further argued that the true perpetrator was probably one of Kaye's many "clients" who was still on the streets of Brighton.

The jury agreed with the defense and acquitted Mancini of all charges.

But the bizarre case of the Brighton Trunk Murders does not end there; Mancini admitted on his deathbed in 1976 that he was in fact responsible for Kaye's death, although he claimed it was an act of self-defense.

The Brighton Trunk Murders truly left an enduring psychological impression on the people of the United Kingdom. For a number of years after the Mancini trial, the British quit referring to their beloved beach getaway as the "Queen of Watering Places" and instead called it the "Queen of Slaughter Places."

Today, the memories of the bizarre string of murderous coincidences that took place in and around Brighton are fading into the distant past. Most of the younger generation does not even know about the Brighton Trunk Murders, and the popular resort town has once again claimed its spot as Britain's prime beachfront vacation spot.

That is, until the next body is found in a trunk near the train station.

CHAPTER 5:

The Abduction and Murder

of Annie Le

America's Ivy League colleges are known for their strict academic requirements and as factories that produce world leaders in the fields of business, science, and politics. The campuses of Ivy League universities are full of history as the halls are named for famous Americans and their architecture is often centuries old. Truly, Ivy League schools are in a world of their own.

The residential neighborhoods that have grown up around the nation's Ivy League schools are usually pretty safe. For instance, Dartmouth is located in the bucolic setting of New Hampshire and Harvard and Princeton are located in low crime suburbs of major cities. Columbia is located in Manhattan, but since the 1990s the crime rate has been very low in that city.

Yale University is a different story.

Yale University, like its Ivy League brothers, is an incredibly fine academic institution that has graduated a number of brilliant minds from around the world; but it is also located in the middle of New Haven, Connecticut.

Since the Puritans first arrived there in the seventeenth century, New Haven has attracted several waves of immigrants. Irish, Italian, and Jewish immigrants immigrated there in large numbers during the nineteenth and early twentieth centuries, and then groups from within the United States, such as blacks from the South, and Puerto Ricans, have moved there in the later twentieth century. The immigrants made New Haven a hard-scrabble, blue collar city that has experienced growing pains over the years.

One of the growing pains New Haven has experienced is a high crime rate.

Gang and drug violence has contributed to place New Haven in the top twenty of the most dangerous American cities per capita, where it enjoys the dubious distinction of being grouped with some of America's more notorious cities, such as Detroit, Chicago, and Memphis. New Haven's high crime rate has been a source of problems for Yale University for a number of years and made national headlines when Yale graduate student Annie Le mysteriously vanished from an on-campus laboratory on September 8, 2009.

A Woman with a Promising Future

In September, 2009, Annie Le was a woman with an incredible future in front of her. At twenty-four years old, Le was a doctoral student of pharmacology who was engaged to be married on September 13. She enjoyed being a student at Yale and was well liked by her friends and colleagues. Le was looking forward to marrying her fiancé Jonathan Widawsky and beginning her life in "the real world."

The petite Le was a highly ambitious young woman who grew up in the San Jose, California area. Le was from a traditional, yet Americanized Vietnamese-American family that placed a high value on education and family, which she dutifully followed in her own life.

From an early age Le showed a keen interest in science and medicine. She volunteered in her community, studied hard, and was always there for family members. Eventually, her hard work paid off, as she graduated as the valedictorian of her high school class and was accepted to the University of Rochester where she earned a BA in bioscience in 2007.

The bright and ambitious Le was then accepted into the pharmacology graduate program at Yale where she was studying enzymes in order to develop treatments for diabetes and cancer.

But all of the hopes and dreams of this bright young woman were needlessly dashed in a bizarre crime that became the focus of national attention.

The Crime

Despite being located in the middle of a high crime city, Yale University is equipped with several levels of security. University police regularly patrol the campus looking for any student in need of help and investigating anything that may seem out of the ordinary. Property crimes have been high at Yale compared to other campuses in the state of Connecticut, but violent assaults and homicides are almost unheard of, which is no doubt at least partially the result of campus police patrols.

Yale University also has other security measures in place to protect its students and staff.

A number of close circuit television cameras strategically placed around the campus record the movements of people in and out of the campus buildings, and many of the buildings can only be accessed with a current Yale University identification card.

Both of the last two security measures played an important role in the Annie Le case.

The morning of September 8 began just as any other for Annie Le. She woke up, had breakfast in her apartment, and then took public transportation to Sterling Hall on Yale's campus where she had an office. She left her purse, phone, and other valuables in her Sterling Hall office and then went to conduct research at the on-campus laboratory around 10 a.m.

Cameras in the laboratory captured images of her entering the building, but not of her leaving.

Le usually returned home in the afternoon, so when she failed to come back to the apartment, her roommate reported her missing around 9 p.m..

Campus, local, and state police, along with the FBI, immediately locked down the campus laboratory and began an exhaustive search for Le. It appeared that one of Yale's brightest stars had been abducted from campus.

The case immediately attracted media attention. A bright, attractive Ivy League student had disappeared from campus with no trace. Le's anguished family and her fiancé appealed to the public for help in press conferences, but as the country watched and hoped for the safe return of the graduate student, some doubted the circumstances.

Some people began to question if she was really abducted and began to propose that maybe she willingly chose to disappear. Perhaps the stress of her rigorous studies combined with doubt about her impending marriage made Le become a runaway bride. Those closest to Le dismissed such theories by pointing out that she only showed hope and excitement for her future and never displayed any signs of doubt towards her marriage. There was no way that Annie Le would have ruined her future and hurt family and friends in such a way, they said. Unfortunately, on September 13, the day of Annie Le's planned wedding, the thoughts of her family and friends were confirmed – the young graduate student's body was discovered in a basement wall of the laboratory.

The Killer

An examination of Le's partially decomposed body revealed that the young woman had been strangled to death and was sexual assaulted. Initially, authorities cast a wide net in their potential suspect pool, which included friends, co-workers, and acquaintances of Le's, but once her body was discovered in the basement of the lab they knew that the killer was someone she worked with.

On the afternoon of September 10, before Le's body was discovered, graduate student Rachel Roth, who also worked in the lab, noticed what appeared to be a blood smear on a box of towels. Roth alerted authorities to the find, and while she waited for police to arrive she noticed twenty-six-year-old lab technician Raymond Clark acting strangely. She said he repositioned the box of towels so that the apparent blood smear was not visible and then cleaned a drain that did not appear to need cleaning.

Clark then told Yale police that he talked to Le in the lab on September 8, but that she left the building just after noon.

The video surveillance clearly showed that Le never left the building, and Raymond quickly became a person of interest in her disappearance. The police also noticed some scratches on Clark's face, but he claimed that he received the injuries from a cat.

Although arrows of suspicion began to clearly point towards Clark early in the investigation, authorities still did not know if they had an abduction, homicide, or runaway bride on their hands.

Further investigation of the laboratory turned up a discarded lab coat that was stained with what was later determined to be blood, some bloody clothing, and work boots with Clark's initials.

Le's body was eventually discovered when the odor from decomposition became apparent to investigators, who then brought in cadaver dogs that located her corpse. Authorities obtained a warrant for Clark's hair, blood, and fingernails on September 15th, which was then matched to some of the items discovered in the lab and on Le's body. The lab technician was arrested on September 17th when he then failed a polygraph examination, which proved to be the final nail in his homicidal coffin.

After a series of pre-trail motions, at the urging of his parents Clark pleaded guilty to Le's murder in March, 2011. The judge sentenced Clark to forty-four years in prison with his release date in the year 2053.

If Clark survives natural causes and the clutches of hardened career criminals, he will be seventy years old when he is released.

Unanswered Questions

The abduction and murder of Annie Le is both a tragic and bizarre tale on so many levels. The tragic nature of the case is obvious: a bright young woman who had so much to offer the world was viciously murdered before her life had a chance to get underway.

The case was bizarre from start to finish.

Her apparent abduction from the supposed safe confines of an Ivy League science lab to the revelation that she was murdered and "hid" inside the lab were all details that make sure this case will never be forgotten.

But perhaps the most mysterious aspect of the case revolves around the killer, particularly what drove Clark to kill Le.

At his sentencing, Clark appeared genuinely contrite as he fought back tears and made a statement to the court.

'Annie was and will always be a wonderful person, by far a better person than I will ever be in my life. I'm sorry I lied. I'm sorry I ruined lives. And I'm sorry for taking Annie Le's life,' said Clark at sentencing.

Despite showing remorse for the horrific act, Clark never told the court why he killed Le.

Raymond Clark was a lab technician who did not get along well with the graduate students and scientists that worked in the lab, as some described him as a "control freak." One lab researcher said that Clark would get upset if others did not follow the smallest rules of the lab, such as wearing shoe covers. "He would make a big deal of it, instead of just requesting that they wear them," said one of the scientists.

Some believe that Clark, a man with limited education who was little more than the laboratory's janitor, felt extremely inadequate around the graduate students and scientists and therefore would make a major issue about minor problems in order to exert some power. On the day he killed Le, Clark sent her a text message requesting a meeting to discuss the sanitary conditions of the cages of the mice that were used for experiments.

Did Le meet with Clark and say something that set the man off into a murderous rage?

If that is the case, there is little in his past to suggest such a thing, and the two worked together for about four months with no signs of turmoil or acrimony. Friends of Clark's were all quick to point out that they were extremely shocked when they learned he murdered Le.

"This is not the Raymond Clark that I know," said Clark's childhood friend Maurice Perry. "I've known him so long. I just can't picture him doing something like this."

Neighbors also described Clark, who lived with his girlfriend and a dog, as thoughtful and considerate.

Yale University president Richard Levin also showed surprise, although his statement was no doubt to at least partially cover himself and the university from a law-suit by Le's family. Levin stated: "His supervisor reports that nothing in the history of his employment at the university gave an indication that his involvement in such a crime might be possible."

Unfortunately, Raymond Clark proved that when it comes to murder, anyone is capable and anything is possible.

An Eerie Footnote

We all know that words we say, if not chosen correctly, can have a tendency to come back to haunt us, but in Annie Le's case, words she *wrote* continue in many ways to haunt Yale's administration.

In February 2009, just months before she was murdered, Annie Le wrote a short article in Yale Medical School's *B Magazine* titled: "Crime and Safety in New Haven." Le's article focused on what Yale students can do to protect themselves from the crime in New Haven.

She wrote: "In short, New Haven is a city, and all cities have their perils, but with a little street smarts, one can avoid becoming another statistic."

Unfortunately for Annie, no amount of street smarts could help her avoid the peril in the laboratory that ultimately made her a statistic.

CHAPTER 6:
The Disappearance of the McStay Family

As detailed in this book, disappearances are not that uncommon and some, such as the vanishing of the Palmer brothers, are downright creepy. No matter how bizarre some missing person cases are, most tend to involve just one person. Whether the person involved got too intoxicated and wandered off, succumbed to the effects of Alzheimer's disease, or was the victim of a homicide, the vast majority of disappearances only involve one person.

Logic and statistics dictate that the chance of more than one person disappearing at the same time from the same place is extremely low. For instance, if a group of people wander from their camp into the wilderness, the chances are pretty good that either one of the campers will be found by a search party or one of the group will make his way back to the camp. The same goes for an abduction-homicide; it is extremely difficult to abduct and murder multiple people at the same time, even if there are multiple killers involved.

These facts are what make the 2010 disappearance of the McStay family in Fallbrook, California both peculiar and frightening.

By all accounts, the McStay family—which was comprised of forty-year-old father Joseph, forty-three-year-old mother Summer, four-year-old boy Gianni, and his three- year-old brother Joe Junior—were an average American family. They lived a relatively comfortable life in a quiet suburban neighborhood that was paid for with the profits from Joe's contracting business and Summer's work as a real estate agent.

The McStays never mentioned to family or friends that they were taking a trip, and they were not known to have any enemies, which is what made their sudden disappearance frightening and the subject of nationwide media attention.

The Disappearance

Joe and Summer never indicated to their friends and family that anything was wrong in their household or that the family was planning on taking any extended trips. In fact, the family had just celebrated Joe Junior's third birthday on January 31, and by all accounts the family appeared happy and content, which made their sudden disappearance all the more mysterious.

After repeated calls from Joe's brother Mike went unanswered, Mike entered the home through a window on February 15 to investigate. The family dogs were in the backyard unfed and there were signs that the family left quickly because food was left out. Mike then called local police to report the strange circumstances and officially begin a missing persons investigation.

The initial police investigation turned up a number of clues, but they only added more mystery to an increasingly enigmatic case.

Although the left out food and the unfed dogs indicated that the McStays left their home in a hurry, there were no signs of a struggle. With the help of Mike and other family members, the police were also able to ascertain that nothing valuable was missing, so a scenario of a home invasion/burglary was quickly ruled out.

The Fallbrook police and San Diego Sheriff's Department quickly canvassed the neighborhood and interviewed all of the McStay's family, friends, and neighbors, which then resulted in a couple of more important clues.

A neighbor's security camera caught images of a car leaving the McStay residence at 7:47 p.m., but the car did not belong to either Joe or Summer! Unfortunately, although technology has come a long way, the resolution of the camera was not good enough to identify the image/s of anyone in the car or the car's license plate. For the time being the mysterious nighttime visitor to the McStay home was a dead end, but it possibly fit part of a bigger picture that had yet to be painted.

The police next interviewed Joe's friend and business partner, Chase Merritt, who said that he received a call from him at 8:28 p.m.. Merritt let the call go to voice mail, as he claimed he often did, because if it was important or work-related then Joe would leave a message.

Joe did not leave a message.

The next major break in the case came on February 8, when the family's Izuzu Trooper was found in the San Ysidro neighborhood of San Diego, which is just north of the international border of the United States and Mexico. The discovery of the McStays' family car was thought to be a big lead, but ultimately raised more questions than there were answers.

Did the McStays simply go to Mexico for a vacation? If so, why did they not tell any of their family or friends? Why did they leave their beloved pets in such a sorry condition? And perhaps the most important question: why would they go to Mexico in the first place?

Tijuana, which is the major Mexican city just south of the border, is a popular destination for many Americans, but it would not be a stretch to say that the city is not exactly family friendly. Tijuana is more known for its brothels, strip clubs, and availability of drugs—both legal and illicit—than it is for any family attractions. Tijuana is clearly not a place where most people would bring two young children.

And why would the family leave their car and walk into Mexico?

There seems to be no reason why they would have done this. Some people argued that perhaps the entire family was trying to get "lost" and moved south of the border to do so, but it no doubt would have been easier to do so with the family car, at least for a while. They could have always sold the car at a later time.

The location of the car on the border raised more questions than there were answers, and many of the McStays' family and friends began to believe that the car was staged at the border by other people, possibly for nefarious reasons.

As family and friends began to doubt that the McStays were in Mexico, police uncovered another clue that once more turned the investigation upside down. A forensic search of the family's computer revealed that on January 28, internet searches were made about travel in Mexico, specifically what type of documentation children would need to enter the country.

Perhaps the McStays, for whatever reason, simply had enough of life in America and decided to leave on a whim to Mexico. After all, Summer and Joe were known to be free spirits, so maybe the situation was not so nefarious.

Or maybe they had to leave town quickly for more ominous reasons.

The McStays' family and friends remained unconvinced that Joe and Summer would have taken their children to another country without telling anyone, but without more evidence there was little that the police could do.

The disappearance of the McStay family would remain one of the most highly reported missing persons cases in recent American history.

Media Attention and Investigation

As the clues and circumstances of the disappearance of the McStay family emerged, the situation became one made for the media. Images of the attractive couple and their cute little boys were repeatedly flashed across television screens, newspaper articles, and webpages.

The case quickly came to the attention of one-man crime crusader John Walsh, who hosted the popular weekly show *America's Most Wanted*. Walsh's show profiled notorious criminals who were on the run, as well as missing children, which Walsh often became emotional about since his own son was abducted and murdered by a serial killer in 1981. The McStay family disappearance seemed tailor-made for *America's Most Wanted*, so the case was profiled on a June 2010 episode. A number of viewers called into the tip line after the episode aired, but unfortunately they all turned out to be dead ends.

The McStay case was also featured on the similarly themed show, *Unsolved Mysteries,* hosted by late actor Dennis Farina, but again, the tips that were generated led nowhere.

As the months that the McStay family was missing turned into years, the police, John Walsh, and Dennis Farina were not the only people investigating their disappearance; former radio talk show host and author Rick Baker also threw his hat into the ring.

Baker began investigating the case independently from the police shortly after the family went missing. He interviewed friends, family, and potential witnesses and came to some interesting conclusions in his book, *No Goodbyes: The Mysterious Disappearance of the McStay Family.* Baker's interest in the case began when he interviewed Mike McStay on his San Diego radio show in 2011. After the radio interview with McStay, Baker compiled a list of potential sightings of the family and followed up on them, which took the radio host throughout Latin America.

Four days after the McStays vanished, a video of a family of four crossing the U.S.-Mexican border on foot surfaced, but it could not be determined who they were. After that report, more and more tips of sightings in countries such as the Dominican Republic, Belize, and Haiti kept a glimmer of hope alive for the friends and family of the McStays.

Baker packed his suitcases and went to a number of the exotic locales to follow up on the leads. "I've traveled around the world to what I thought were verified sightings," said Baker, but ultimately none of them panned out.

The supposed Latin American connection led many to believe that violent drug cartels may have been responsible for the family's abduction, even though there were no signs that either of the parents owed drug debts. There was also no evidence that apart from some occasional marijuana use either of the McStay parents ever took "harder" drugs such as cocaine, methamphetamines, or heroin. Joe and Summer McStay just did not fit the profile of drug cartel victims.

The location of the McStay's Izuzu also did not seem like the work of a drug cartel to Baker. "Why did they stage the car? A cartel is not interested in staging anything," said Baker.

Baker's observation is correct in regards to cartel activities south of the border, but it is commonly known that the cartels keep more of a low profile in the United States and refrain from some of their more blatant acts of extreme violence. With that said, it does seem like a lot of effort for gang members to go through to somehow cover up the abduction of a middle class American family.

As Baker's independent investigation continued, the police began to focus on a suspect who was right under their noses.

A Suspect Emerges

Charles "Chase" Merritt, now fifty-nine years old, was a friend and occasional business associate of Joe. The two men worked on a number of projects in the area installing fountains, which was Joe's specialty, and were generally known to get along well.

Decorative water fountains that are often seen in the yards and driveways of expensive homes are what Joe specialized in and how he was able to provide for his family. Business slowed during 2008 and 2009, as it did for the entire construction industry nationwide, but at the time of the McStay family disappearance business was picking back up. Joe was finally able to start saving some money again for his family, and he was also able to hire more employees and give some work to his friends such as Charles Merritt.

Although Merritt and McStay did not spend too much time together outside of work—after all, Joe had a family to look after—by all accounts they got along fairly well and considered each other colleagues and friends. Also, a large part of Merritt's income was derived from work McStay sent his way, so at first glance it seemed unlikely that he would have anything to do with Joe and his family's disappearance.

But Merritt was the last known person to see Joe.

Merritt told police that he met Joe at a Chick-fil-A restaurant in the afternoon to discuss some potential future contracts and receive payment for some completed jobs. He claimed that McStay seemed fine and that the two left and went their separate ways after the brief meeting. As the last person to see Joe McStay, a certain amount of suspicion was cast Merritt's way, but that alone is not enough to arrest someone for a crime, which is if a crime in fact took place.

But it turns out that Merritt also had a bit of a shady past.

Merritt was a convicted felon who had a rap sheet that included burglary and possession of stolen property. His last conviction came in 2001. Although Merritt had a criminal record, all of his convictions were for non-violent offenses and no one that knew him indicated that he was capable of abducting four people. He was not known as a violent person and had no known altercations with Joe.

The case into the disappearance of the McStay family continued to go off into several directions, and as time went by media interest began to wane. Many in the McStay family began to question if they would ever know what happened to their loved ones.

Then on November 13, 2013, the case took an unfortunate turn.

The Discovery

San Bernardino County in southern California is the largest county in land mass in the United States. Although the county is also quite populated, with over two million inhabitants, most of those people live in towns such as San Bernardino, which are just outside of Los Angeles County in the far western end of the county. Once you get east of San Bernardino, the county is a vast sea of desert and mountains that stretches all the way to the state lines of Nevada and Arizona.

It is exactly the type of place where a person can easily go missing, alive or dead.

On November 13, a motorcyclist discovered the remains of the entire McStay family in two shallow graves outside of the town of Victorville. The search for the McStays was finally over, but the case then evolved into a homicide investigation.

Although the bodies had apparently been in the ground since the time of their disappearance, the dry desert climate preserved the bodies of the adults quite well. An autopsy determined that the parents, and more than likely the children as well, were killed by blunt force trauma to the head, although the bodies of the children were too degraded to tell for sure. A sledge hammer recovered from one of the graves was probably the murder weapon.

Charles Merritt was arrested the next day for the family's murder and in pre-trial hearings it was revealed that the police had amassed a mountain of evidence on him during their investigation.

Much of the evidence against Merritt is circumstantial, but it is voluminous and appears quite damning.

The investigation into Merritt's background discovered that the contractor with a modest income liked to spend several days at a time in the area casinos.

And Merritt was not winning!

To pay for his gambling losses, Merritt wrote over $21,000 in checks on Joe McStay's business account and then cancelled McStay's QuickBooks accounting membership on February 8, 2010, the day the McStay's Izuzu was discovered near the international border.

The circumstantial evidence against Merritt further piled up when it was discovered that he withdrew thousands more from Joe's business account during the period from February 9, 2010, well into March, to pay for extended trips to area casinos.

Merritt's DNA was also recovered from the family's Izuzu, which can certainly be argued away as he was an associate's of Joes, but when taken with the other evidence, looks to be the final straw in the camel's back of circumstantial evidence.

Merritt now sits in the San Bernardino County jail and faces the death penalty if he is convicted. Perhaps in an effort to stall the inevitable, Merritt has fired five different attorneys, which has caused considerable delay to the trial. Although the surviving members of the McStay family are glad that an arrest has been made, the loss of their loved ones will always weigh heavy on their hearts.

Although it looks like all arrows point towards Charles Merritt as the killer, some doubt if he is the sole perpetrator. One argument is that it would be too difficult for one person to kill four people, even if two of them were children. The reality is that Joe trusted his business associate and he therefore never saw him coming, so to speak. Once the McStay parents knew what was happening, they probably complied in order to save their children and by the time they got to the desert outside Victorville, it was too late.

In a case as strange as the McStay family disappearance, conspiracy theories are bound to take hold, and even if Merritt is convicted and put to death, some will continue to doubt that all the facts have come to light.

The true tragedy of the McStay murder case is that they were murdered by someone they trusted who killed them for the oldest motive known to man—greed.

CHAPTER 7:
The Rayna Rison Murder

In recent years, cold cases that were solved through advances in science have been featured on popular documentary television shows such as *Forensic Files* and *The New Detectives*. These shows stress the unbiased nature of DNA in contrast to the often un-credible accounts of witnesses. The reality is that many criminals are smart enough to leave no traces of physical evidence. Crafty criminals often wear gloves to conceal their fingerprints and destroy the bodies of murder victims in order to destroy any physical evidence that could point towards their guilt. Bodies are also often moved from the scene of the murder to another location by the murderer in efforts to confuse homicide investigators. And sometimes criminals just get lucky and no physical evidence is left at the crime scene, or what little was, has been degraded by the time forensic investigators find it.

Because of the sometimes crafty nature of killers, oftentimes investigators are forced to rely upon the age old evidence of eye-witness testimony. The problem with eye witnesses is that humans can be notoriously unreliable at times. People might be scared to offer testimony, or they may feel some sort of misplaced loyalty toward a criminal.

But sometimes, if given enough time, circumstances and a guilty conscience will lead to unknown or once thought unreliable witnesses to help solve a murder.

This is what happened in the 1993 murder case of Rayna Rison.

A Promising Future

Located about an hour's drive east of Chicago on Interstate 80, LaPorte County, Indiana, is known for its low crime, affordable housing, and generally being a good place to live. The people of LaPorte County take pride in their homes and schools and are known for being friendly, helpful people.

Sixteen-year-old Rayna Rison was one of LaPorte's friendly inhabitants.

Rayna enjoyed spending time with her parents, Bernie and Karen, and she was particularly close to her sister Wendy, who was one year her junior. Rayna excelled in school and was known to be a popular girl who got along with most of the disparate cliques that are often found in American high schools.

In her spare time, Rayna worked part-time at the Pine Lake animal clinic in the town of LaPorte. The veterinarians she worked for stated she had a natural gift for the position and would no doubt someday realize her dream of becoming a veterinarian and opening her own clinic.

But that dream was shattered when she vanished from the animal clinic on the night of March 26, 1993.

When Rayna failed to come home that night her parents and sister began to worry. The responsible sixteen-year-old always checked in with her parents, especially if she stayed all night at a friend's. Rayna's parents called around to her friends, but no one had seen her.

It was if she had vanished into thin air.

The local police and sheriff's department soon got involved, and the search for Rayna Rison became a missing person case.

The Search for Rayna

Friends and family of Rayna joined together with local law enforcement to find her by searching local ponds, rivers, and fields. Her family also plastered the area with flyers that had recent pictures of Rayna. The extensive search quickly paid off when Rayna's car was located a day after her disappearance in a rural area of LaPorte County, but there were no signs of Rayna.

An examination of Rayna's car seemed to reveal nothing that could help investigators: there was no blood present, and there was no damage to the car. It was as if she simply drove the car to that location and then left it for whatever reason. The discovery of the car raised a lot of red flags, but the local police were quick to point out that at that point they only had a missing person case on their hands.

The disappearance frightened residents of LaPorte County and also brought media attention to the area.

Rayna's disappearance was featured three times by John Walsh on *America's Most Wanted* in just one month, and Oakland Athletics owner and part time LaPorte resident, Charlie Finley, offered a $25,000 reward for Rayna's safe return.

To some outside LaPorte County, Finley's interest in the case appeared to be grandstanding, but the locals knew he was sincere. Yes, the billionaire had a tendency to be flamboyant at times—one of his best known accomplishments was bringing the rock band The Beatles to Kansas City during their limited American tour in 1964—but he also had a legitimate love for LaPorte County. Finley donated much of his money to support schools in the county and even lived in the area while he owned the Athletics. But despite the immense media attention, profiles on *America's Most Wanted*, and the reward offered from Finley's own pockets, the police received no credible leads as to Rayna's whereabouts.

Then, about a month after her car was discovered, the body of Rayna Rison was found in a lake in LaPorte County.

The investigation then shifted from that of a missing person case to a homicide, but unfortunately for the authorities, the fact that Rayna's body was submerged in water for so long meant that it would be more difficult to lift forensic evidence from the scene or Rayna's body.

The autopsy determined that Rayna died of strangulation, and although DNA profiling was becoming more widely used by law enforcement in 1993, no forensic evidence was taken from her body. Police could not even say for sure if she was killed at the location where she was discovered or dumped at the scene. There were also *apparently* no eye witnesses to the murder.

Who would kill such an innocent girl?

The Case Goes Cold

As time moved further away from the discovery of Rayna's body, her murder began to slowly fade from the public eye. Her family held vigils every year and her case had an occasional mention on *America's Most Wanted*, but by 1998 it seemed as though the killer would never be caught.

But then an arrest was made.

Rayna's brother-in-law Ray McCarty, who was twenty-eight at the time of her murder, was arrested and charged with the killing in 1998.

Lori McCarty, who was married to Ray, was Rayna's older sister, and although there was a considerable age difference between the two, the younger sister often spent a lot of time around the McCarty house. Rayna also became close with Ray—too close.

When Ray was twenty-four, he began molesting twelve-year-old Rayna, which resulted in a pregnancy when the girl was just thirteen. McCarty used the typical method of operation of a child predator by first appearing as a friend to Rayna and then using a combination of compliments and threats to sexually molest her. He was eventually convicted of molesting Rayna, served time in jail, and was then placed on probation. The local police were particularly interested in the fact that McCarty threatened Rayna and her parents' lives if she ever revealed the truth of his despicable acts.

She did report him and was later murdered.

Almost immediately, McCarty was the top suspect. Besides his past crimes and threats against Rayna, he was unable to account for his whereabouts during the time Rayna was abducted. Despite the circumstantial evidence against

McCarty, there was no physical evidence and no eye-witness that could place him with Rayna the day she disappeared.

Perhaps feeling a bit of pressure, the LaPorte county prosecutor's office charged McCarty with murder in 1998, but released him fifteen months later when it was clear there was not enough evidence to convict him.

Investigators either had to find more evidence against McCarty or look for new suspects.

Was Rayna the victim of a local serial killer?

Larry Dewayne Hall was described by many as polite and mild mannered, yet beneath the calm exterior lurked a raging serial killer. Larry Hall was a native of Wabash, Indiana, who worked as a janitor and enjoyed taking part in Civil War reenactments in his free time.

He also enjoyed killing women.

Hall confessed to killing a number of women, and some authorities believe the count may be as high as forty. They think that as he traveled the country taking part in battle reenactments, he was also killing women. So far, Hall has not garnered as much attention as other more well-known serial killers, but that may change if more murders are definitively attributed to him.

In 2010, a book written by Christopher Martin titled *Urges: A Chronicle of Serial Killer Larry Hall* was published that argued

Hall may be Rison's killer. He pointed out that Hall and McCarty knew each other in grade school, which suggested that there may have been collusion in Rayna's murder. Martin also stated that a police search of Hall's home turned up a box of birth control pills with Rayna Rison's name on it, although investigators said that none of the drug stores in the area had a prescription for Rison.

He was also apparently out of the area doing a reenactment when Rayna disappeared.

It was never explained why Hall had those pills in his possession, but some investigators believe it was part of one of the killer's sick fantasies. Hall, like many other people in Indiana, simply followed Rayna's case and got some sort of perverse pleasure out of fantasizing about the details of her death. LaPorte County authorities were adamant that there was no way Hall was Rison's killer.

To the public, it seemed as though Rayna's killer, or killers, may never be caught. But behind the scenes, as Martin was attempting to finger Hall, the police were about to nab the killer.

Old Loyalties are Shattered

The criminal underworld is an interesting place. Yes, there is a criminal code where it is a big no-no to be a "snitch" or informant for the police, but it is also a society where every man is out for himself; loyalties are often tenuous and subject to change depending on the situation a criminal may find himself in, such as the capricious nature of his cohorts. A criminal who is tight-lipped and loyal to another person at one time may find that loyalty detrimental to his own life in the future.

The criminal underworld is also a domain driven by fear.

Some of the most successful criminals keep their underlings under control through extreme acts of violence that are perpetrated either on others for the underlings to see, or on the underlings themselves. A criminal is less inclined to give the police information on one of his associates if the person is known to employ extreme violence against his enemies.

In the cold case murder of Rayna Rison, the crime was ultimately solved not through forensic evidence, but by the police breaking through the warped sense of loyalty and violence that pervades the criminal underworld.

Thirty-eight-year old Jason Tibbs was arrested in August 2013 for the murder of Rayna Rison. The arrest came as a surprise to many in LaPorte County who expected her killer to be an outsider like Dewayne Hall, but it turns out that he was in fact at the top of the suspect list at the beginning of the investigation.

At the time of Rayna's disappearance and murder, Tibbs was eighteen and had briefly dated Rison. It was quickly determined that Tibbs still held a flame for Rayna as indicated in letters that he wrote to her in which he said he would "go to almost any extreme" to date her again. A ring that was identified as belonging to Tibbs was also found in Rayna's abandoned car.

Also, in the years after Rayna's murder, Tibbs developed a reputation as a violent thug in LaPorte County.

When Rayna's sister and former classmates graduated from high school and went on to start careers and families, Jason Tibbs graduated from the school of hard knocks. Tibbs had encounters with the police throughout the 1990s and was known as a tough guy within the local criminal underworld. A combination of fear and misplaced loyalty helped protect Tibbs from justice for two decades, but time began running out for him in 2008.

Ricky Hammons was fourteen when Rayna Rison was murdered. Like Tibbs, he was a bit of a juvenile delinquent who enjoyed skipping school and smoking pot, and also like Tibbs he immersed himself in the LaPorte County's criminal underworld during the 1990s. In 1999, at the age of twenty, Hammons shot and killed a man in rural LaPorte, which landed him in the Wabash, Indiana, state prison with a forty-five year sentence.

Life had not gone well for Ricky Hammons.

Then in 2008, for reasons that are debated, Hammons reached out to LaPorte County detectives with information in the cold case murder of Rayna Rison. Tibbs' attorneys argued that Hammons made up the information for a reduction to his sentence but LaPorte County prosecutor denied that stating, "There was no deal with a witness despite the suggestion there was."

A man has a lot of time to contemplate his life behind bars.

Perhaps feelings of remorse and sympathy for the Rison family combined with no reason to fear Tibbs anymore made Hammons come forward. It may also be that he just wanted to get even with Tibbs for some reason. Tibbs was known to intimidate and bully younger delinquents in LaPorte County, so maybe Hammons finally saw his chance to get even. Regardless of his reasons, Hammons statements to LaPorte County investigators quickly got the ball rolling that led to Tibbs' arrest.

Hammons told the authorities that on the night of March 26, 1993, he was smoking marijuana in the hayloft of a pole barn when a car pulled in that was driven by his sister's boyfriend, Eric Freeman, with Jason Tibbs along as passenger. He said that Tibbs then opened the trunk of the car where he could see what appeared to be a body wrapped in a blanket. Freeman argued with Tibbs over what happened before Hammons then snuck out of the barn.

Although Hammons' statement appeared to verify what many LaPorte County investigators originally thought, more evidence was needed to corroborate his story in order to make an arrest. The next step was to locate Eric Freeman.

Locating Eric Freeman was easy, as he too was incarcerated on a murder conviction.

Where it is possible that Ricky Hammons may have been driven by a combination of remorse and sympathy to come forward with information in the murder of Rayna Rison, Eric Freeman was clearly driven by fear, the fear of spending the rest of his life in prison.

Although Freeman is currently serving time in prison for murder, he, like most murderers, will probably be paroled someday. The likelihood of him ever being released would be severely diminished if he was convicted of another murder, so Freeman quickly decided to talk under one condition, that he receive immunity from prosecution for the murder or Rayna Rison.

Unlike in movies and television shows, prosecutors in the real world are usually loathe to award full immunity to criminals in order to obtain their testimony in court. Shaving a few years off an impending sentence is standard, but sometimes full immunity is awarded if the person in question played a significantly lesser role in the crime or there are other mitigating circumstances.

Serving time on a previous murder conviction is clearly a mitigating circumstance since Freeman was going nowhere anytime soon.

Freeman's statement to police and subsequent testimony at Tibbs' murder trial corroborated Hammons' statement and also filled in some important details.

According to Freeman, he rode with Tibbs to the Pine Lake animal clinic so that Tibbs could speak with Rayna and hopefully persuade her to start dating him again. The conversation quickly turned into an argument as Rison was adamant that she did not want to date Tibbs as she was seeing someone else.

Despite Freeman's testimony, the next part of the story remains somewhat enigmatic. For some reason, after she had a heated conversation with Tibbs, Rayna agreed to get into the car with him and Freeman. Freeman then said that he drove the two to a rural area where their argument continued until Tibbs realized he could not win so he then overpowered the girl and strangled her to death. The two men then put Rayna's body in the trunk of the car and drove to the barn to contemplate their next move. It was at this point that Hammons saw Freeman and Tibbs.

After a heated argument over what he had done, Tibbs convinced Freeman to help him dispose of Rayna's body. Freeman claimed he helped Tibbs because he feared going to prison and what the killer might do to him. He also felt a sense of loyalty to his troubled friend. But nearly twenty years later, Freeman feared spending the rest of his life in prison more than his former friend.

On November 7, 2014, primarily due to the testimonies of Hammons and Freeman, Jason Tibbs was found guilty of the murder of Rayna Rison and sentenced to forty years in prison. Under the Indiana Department of Corrections parole system, Tibbs will probably serve just under twenty years.

Despite the length of the saga to bring Rayna's killer to justice and what many believed was too lenient of a sentence for Tibbs, the Rison family has finally found some peace and closure.

"Hopefully now my family can find some semblance of peace from what we've been through for the last twenty years," said Rayna's father, Ben Rison.

CHAPTER 8:
The Murder of Sara Lynn Wineski

The murder cases that grab the most headlines tend to be ones where the victims are truly "innocent" and in the wrong place and the wrong time. Part of the shock in those types of cases comes from the sense that no matter how safe a neighborhood one may live in, there is always the potential to be the victim of a heinous crime. Indeed, it is relatively rare, even in cities with high crime rates, for people not involved in criminal activity to be murdered.

When people do hear about criminals and people from the lowest rungs of society being murdered, the response is often differential at best. The philosophy holds that the police are here to protect law abiding citizens, not the criminals and other assorted "scum."

But the reality is that the police are here to protect all members of society, no matter what a person's situation currently is. No one is disposable and every life has value, even the lives of criminals and prostitutes.

The best police officers around the world hold this attitude, which was put into action by the St. Petersburg, Florida, Police Department when they discovered the body of forty- nine-year-old prostitute Sara Lynn Wineski.

Around 11 p.m. on May 21, 2005, residents who were staying at the St. Petersburg Ronald McDonald House were awoken up by sounds of screams. Oftentimes in large American cities such sounds go unnoticed, but possibly because of the proximity of the Ronald McDonald House, a resident called the police. The police responded to the scene, but after they saw no signs of an assault or other criminal activity they moved on to other calls.

The next day, the body of Sarah Lynn Wineski was discovered under a deck of the Ronald McDonald House. She had been raped and strangled to death, but other than the ear witness who called into the police the night of the murder, there were no witnesses to the crime.

Police immediately suspected that Wineski, who was homeless and had been working as a prostitute, fell victim to a serial rapist who had been operating in the area. A background check of Wineski revealed that she was new to the Tampa Bay and knew few people, so it was believed that she did not know her killer. Random murders are the toughest to solve, but the St. Petersburg police had one powerful piece of evidence that the killer left behind—his DNA profile.

But the police needed a suspect to link the DNA to, which could take years or might never happen at all.

Sara Lynn Wineski

Sometimes it is easy to write off and forget about crime victims like Sara Wineski. We tend not to give a second thought when crime happens to criminals, the homeless, or those who live "on the other side of town", and when they become victims little is usually said. Sometimes, these people get mentioned in the local press but are often never named. Wineski's killing probably would have been glossed over in the local Tampa Bay press as well, if it were not for the location of her murder. A murder at the Ronald McDonald House, where family members of children undergoing treatment for serious illnesses stay, surely gave unfavorable attention to St. Petersburg.

When she was murdered, Sara Wineski had hit rock bottom. Her life had spiraled out of control through a series of bad relationships, drug use, and criminal activity, but things were not always that way. Wineski was a mother of four and had four grandchildren, and her family still loved her despite her plethora of demons.

"We have wonderful memories of her," said Candice Chessman, one of Wineski's daughters. "And her murderer stole the hope that we all carried in our hearts that we would have the chance to make more memories with her someday."

Wineski had only recently arrived in the Tampa Bay area in an effort to get a fresh start, but with no money or contacts in the area she quickly turned to her old drug habits and prostitution. Prostitution was an easy and quick way for Wineski to make money for her drug habit, although it ultimately was the source of her final demise.

Much of society may have given up on Sara Lynn Wineski, but the St. Petersburg police did not.

A DNA Match

The homicide detectives of the St. Petersburg police department were just as dedicated to catching the killer of Sara Lynn Wineski as any other murderer, and they knew that the small bit of DNA they lifted from Wineski's body would probably be the key to catching him.

Chances are someone who would commit such a terrible crime had either done so before or would again at some point in the future. Despite that grim prospect, it meant that there was a good chance of eventually catching Wineski's killer. The police entered Wineski's killer's DNA sample into the Combined DNA Index System (CODIS) and waited for a match. The CODIS database was established after the DNA Identification Act became law in 1994. CODIS is an FBI program, but samples are taken from all fifty states, the federal government, and the District of Colombia. At first, samples were taken from convicted sex offenders in various states, but over the years the database has grown to include persons convicted of all felonies, and in some states, those even charged with felonies and some misdemeanors. Each individual state determines its own criteria for who is required to give DNA samples, but by 2006 every state had joined the CODIS database on some level.

2006 also happened to be the year when the DNA from Wineski's body was matched to a suspect!

In many ways, the trajectory of Raymond Samuels' life was similar to Wineski's. He suffered from a variety of personal issues, was a drug user, and was homeless and only in the Tampa Bay area for a very short time when Wineski was murdered. But unlike Wineski, Samuels chose to take out his rage on others.

The DNA taken from Wineski's body was definitively matched to Samuels.

It turns out that Samuels was easy to locate. In 2006, he was incarcerated in an Ohio prison with a lengthy sentence for a violent home invasion of an elderly couple. When Samuels entered the Ohio Department of Corrections after his conviction, a sample of his DNA profile was taken and entered into the CODIS database.

Detective Mike Kovacsev of the St. Petersburg police department had not given up on finding Sara Wineski's killer and routinely took the time to enter the DNA of the unknown male taken from the victim into the CODIS database. In late 2006, they matched the sample to Samuels, but waited several more years to charge him.

There were still too many questions that had to be answered before formal charges could be brought, foremost whether Samuels and Wineski knew each other. After all, Wineski was a known prostitute and the DNA sample taken from her body may have been the result of a consensual, paid sexual encounter. Kovacsev and other detectives from St. Petersburg traveled to Ohio to interview Samuels, but the convict asserted his Fifth Amendment right and refused to talk.

Kovacsev was confident that he had his man and kept the Wineski family continually updated about the case.

"The family was understanding," said Kovacsev. "It's not like we had someone out on the street. He was in custody so he wasn't going anywhere."

Forensic technicians ran more tests on the DNA recovered from the scene to make sure they had the right man and, most importantly, they were also able to match DNA taken from a belt believed to be the murder weapon to Samuels.

Samuels was charged with first degree murder in the death of Sara Wineski in 2013 and currently sits in the Pinellas County jail in Florida awaiting trial.

Wineski's family is grateful that Kovacsev and the other detectives from St. Petersburg did not forget about their loved one, despite her past.

"As a family, we are not in denial about where she was in life, but it is important to us that people know that her life was not a waste and not something anyone had the right to take from her," said Candice Chessman. "She was not always homeless and alone."

CHAPTER 9:
The Murder of Little Anna Palmer

As detailed in the last story, the murder of anyone, no matter his or her background, is always a terrible thing. But the murder of a child clearly brings out a slew of emotions in even the most stoic of people.

What type of person could kill an innocent child? This is a question that psychiatrists, psychologists, and penal experts have attempted to answer now for decades through interviews and examinations of known child killers. Unfortunately, all the studies have apparently failed to unlock the secrets to what makes a child killer tick because the murder of children keeps happening.

With that said, child murder is still a relatively rare phenomenon, and children who follow basic safety rules are usually exempt from the worst category of criminals, which makes the next case all the more frightening.

In 1998, ten-year-old Anna Palmer was like any other kid her age—she liked to spend time with her friends, pets, and family. Most importantly, Anna followed her mother's safety rules, but none of that helped the poor little girl when she was brutally murdered on her family's porch in broad daylight on September 10, 1998.

The Crime

September 10th began just like any other in the Palmer household in Salt Lake City, Utah. At around 5 p.m., Anna called her mother Nancy at work to ask if she could play outside with some neighborhood kids. The Palmer's neighborhood was very safe and everyone knew each other, so it was common for all the kids to meet up and ride bikes or play games like hide and seek. Fifth grader Anna was allowed to take part in the neighborhood activities as long as she told her mother where she was going and came back home at a specific time, usually before dark. Nancy told Anna that it would be fine, but that she should be home by 7 p.m. when she arrived home from work.

When Nancy came home at 7, she was surprised to see Anna lying on the front porch, but when she got closer her surprise turned to horror—little Anna was stiff and in a pool of blood. The petrified mother immediately called 911 and attempted to conduct CPR on Anna, but the poor little girl's throat was gashed and her spinal cord was severed. Anna was dead before Nancy got home.

An autopsy revealed that Anna was beaten and stabbed five times. Either the gash to the throat or the stab to the spinal cord could have killed her. Anna was also sexually assaulted.

After the initial shock of the horrific murder wore off, the mood of the residents of Salt Lake City turned to fear and anger. If such a despicable murder could happen to a girl that seemingly followed all the safety rules and who lived in a safe neighborhood, then no child was safe. The people were also angry, and in the religiously conservative state of Utah, people had biblical retribution on their minds.

The Salt Lake City police had to move fast to catch Anna's killer.

The Investigation

Homicide detectives with the Salt Lake City police department immediately went to work by canvassing Anna's neighborhood and interviewing her friends and family. The case was as bizarre as it was heart wrenching due to the circumstances of little Anna being abducted and murdered all within a matter of minutes, near a busy intersection, and during daylight hours. Despite those facts, no one had seen her taken or murdered.

Or did they?

Detectives quickly put together a timeline for the last two hours of Anna Palmer's life, which helped bring to light a suspect.

After she got off the phone with her mother, Anna walked a few houses down to meet her friend Loxane Konesavanh. The two girls went to a local park and spent most of the next two hours swinging. When it got close to 7 p.m., Anna, being the safe girl who followed her mother's rules, began to walk back home with Loxane. The two girls then noticed that a man was following them, so remembering "stranger danger," they let him pass and said nothing to him. Loxane said that when the man passed them, he turned and glared at Anna.

The two girls then stopped at the yard of fourteen-year-old Amie Johnson to see her new kitten. Loxane then went home a different way than Anna, but Anna was apparently accompanied by the man the two girls had seen before.

"He creeped me out personally," said Johnson, who witnessed the mysterious man walking with Anna. "I looked back and Anna was walking home, and he was still walking behind her like a crazy person. I looked again and no one was there."

Adult neighbors also reported seeing a young man who fit the girls' description lurking around the area earlier in the day. Witnesses said he looked drugged or drunk, but none knew who he was. A man matching the description was also seen walking around the scene of Anna's murder.

Did the killer return to the scene of the crime?

The lead sounded promising to investigators, but identifying the creepy stranger would prove to be extremely difficult. Detectives interviewed everyone who lived in the neighborhood and paid special attention to all known sex offenders. In total, the Salt Lake City Police Department interviewed over 200 people in connection with the murder of Anna Palmer.

Anna's family also got involved by making public appeals via the media for anyone with any information about the little girl's murder to come forward to the police. Further incentive was added with an $11,000 reward for information leading to the killer's arrest and conviction, but still no one came forward. The case quickly became cold.

Although the case may have gone cold, little Anna took an important clue from the killer that ultimately led to his arrest. Despite her size, the little girl ferociously fought her attacker by scratching him, which left some of the killer's DNA profile under her fingernails.

1998 was still early in terms of the CODIS database, but forensic experts with the Salt Lake City police dutifully collected a sample where it would be entered at a later time.

Matt Breck

In 1998, California native Matt Breck was nineteen with no direction in his life. He originally came to Utah with his brother

Tom after Tom's friend, Todd Clark, told the two that they could find steady employment and a chance to start over in the Beehive State. Not long after they arrived in Utah, Tom found steady employment, but things did not go that way for Matt.

Clark said Breck thought of himself as a tough guy who would rather spend the day drinking than working. He also said that Breck tried to pick fights with people and liked to carry knives, which he proudly showed to anyone interested. Clark's wife was particularly creeped out by the younger Breck and claims she told a police officer she knew to take a look at Matt when she heard about Anna's murder. Around the time Anna was murdered, Breck was charged with a violent felony in an unrelated case, but had the charged lowered to misdemeanor and served very little time in jail.

Most importantly, no DNA was taken from Breck during his short stay in the county jail.

After he got out of jail in Utah, Breck headed north to Idaho, but instead of getting a new start, his criminal behavior got more extreme. He was convicted of a burglary charge in 1999, served two years, and was released in 2001. Not long after his release, he was picked up on a child molestation charge and given a lengthy prison sentence.

A sample of his DNA was also taken and entered into the CODIS database.

The CODIS system needs to be constantly updated, and agencies that are looking for a match from a DNA sample need to continually check the system—emails are not sent when/if a match is made.

In late 2009, detectives from Salt Lake City finally received the news they were waiting for—a match had been made in the CODIS system to the DNA recovered from under Anna's fingernails. Authorities then went to the Idaho prison where Breck was incarcerated and questioned him about the murder of Anna Palmer. He admitted that he lived in the neighborhood at the time, but denied involvement in her murder or of even knowing the little girl. It was at that point that police knew they had their man.

Breck was then extradited to Salt Lake City and charged with first degree murder and aggravated sex abuse of a child. Utah is a death penalty state and if the death penalty was created for any one person, it would be Matthew Breck. Feeling the anger of the residents of Salt Lake City upon him, Breck took the sensible option and pled guilty to murder in 2011 in order to receive a sentence of life without parole.

Some think that Breck got off easy, but the reality is that as a high-profile child killer, his life in a maximum security prison will not be easy. Breck will be sent to one of Utah's tougher prisons where he will probably have to spend most of his life in a protected wing where he will have few luxuries and only be allowed out of his cell for limited periods. If he decides to enter general population, if he even has that option, where he will be afforded more luxuries and freedoms, he then runs the risk of being beaten, raped, or even murdered by any number of inmates. Child killers are at the bottom of any prison hierarchy, which means that Breck will constantly have to watch his back.

Whether Breck chooses to take his chances in the prison's general population or he checks into protective custody, he most certainly has a miserable life ahead of him.

The tragic and strange case of Anna Palmer's murder could only have been solved through scientific advances, namely the CODIS database. As Sam Gill, the district attorney who prosecuted Breck said: "It was through science that this poor girl, who was tragically and horrifically murdered in our community, was able to basically point to her killer."

CHAPTER 10:
The Strange Murder of Roy McCaleb

One does not have to search the internet very long to find stories of spousal murder. The reasons for spousal murder are varied and diverse—greed, jealousy, infidelity, and anger are some of the more common reasons—but sometimes the motive is not so clear and the circumstances are even murkier.

On September 22, 1985, fifty-year-old Ray McCleb was shot to death as he slept in his Houston home. When police arrived at the scene, it appeared to be a case of a burglary gone wrong, but soon after interviewing Ray's wife, forty-three-year-old Carolyn, investigators realized that they were about to embark on a very strange homicide case.

A Carjacking and a Murder

Houston, Texas, is a large American city with typical American problems, crime being at the top of the list. The violent crime rate in Houston is fairly high, but as with most American cities, one can avoid most of the crime by staying out of certain areas. The McCalebs lived in a middle income neighborhood where crime was relatively rare and violent home invasion murders were unheard of. Still, it was the big city and random crime can happen to anyone.

But once homicide investigators took a statement from Carolyn, they began to see that this was no ordinary murder, and it was probably not random. The account that Carolyn McCaleb gave to the police of her husband's murder was so strange that police initially though that it was too bizarre to make up.

According to Carolyn, she was carjacked and raped by a barefoot man with a knife ten days before her husband was murdered and then, somehow, the rapist learned her address and came back.

On the night Roy was murdered, Carolyn claimed that the rapist came into her room where he tortured and raped her for some time before he found the pistol that she kept under her pillow. The rapist then went into Roy's room, who was heavily sedated from a recent back surgery and also convalescing from a heart attack, and shot him in the head at point blank range in total darkness. The killer then ran for the door when he bumped into Carolyn and dropped the gun, which she then picked up and fired two shots at him, but missed.

Obviously, the story had more holes in it than a slice of Swiss cheese, but the inconsistencies continued to pile up and cast even more suspicion in Carolyn's direction.

The first question that police asked Carolyn was why she did not report the rape and carjacking that supposedly took place ten days prior to her husband's murder. With a straight face and in a calm demeanor, Carolyn simply said that she did not want to upset her husband who was recovering from recent health problems. The answer was suspicious, but suspicion alone is not enough for an arrest, so police began to investigate the carjacker story.

Almost immediately, homicide detectives had a difficult time locating a suspect in the crime because Carolyn's description of the killer was not consistent. In fact, Carolyn said the killer-rapist was white in her first statement, but then later said the assailant was black. When asked how she could get such an important and major detail wrong, she said that being in the south, she was embarrassed and did not want people to think she had an affair with her attacker.

Other details of Carolyn's account of the murder simply did not add up.

Carolyn, Ray, and the supposed killer were not the only people in the McCaleb house that night. Carolyn's son from a previous marriage and his girlfriend were also present when the murder took place. Neither saw an intruder in the home, although both were awake at the time Carolyn claims he made his getaway.

Then there was her behavior after the police arrived.

Carolyn's account was described as rehearsed and for the most part terse. She then took a shower, even though she was explicitly told that doing so would damage any physical evidence from the rape. Although she did go to the hospital after her interview with police, she left before doctors could perform a thorough examination. Finally, she refused to take a polygraph examination.

To most people in the Houston area it appeared that Carolyn was her husband's killer, but despite the circumstantial evidence, Harris County prosecutors were unwilling to charge her without some tangible, physical evidence.

It would be a long time before Ray McCaleb's killer was brought to justice.

The Years Pass By

As the years after Ray McCaleb's murder turned into decades, the case slipped out of the minds of most Houstonians, but the Harris County prosecutors did not forget. Although there was a plethora of physical evidence in this case—they had the murder weapon and the body of the victim—the circumstances prohibited the prosecutors from charging

98

Carolyn. Yes, her story sounded phony, but they had nothing to prove otherwise. But that did not stop the prosecutors from working on the case. A succession of prosecutors continued to quietly keep the case open.

And they were not looking for the mysterious barefoot rapist.

Carolyn was the authorities' only suspect from the beginning, and as they researched the woman's past, they were astonished with what they found!

It turns out that Ray was Carolyn's eighth husband, and she was still legally married to her seventh when Ray was murdered. It turns out that when she left husband number seven for Ray, she took the unlucky guy's $4,000 tax refund check for good measure. The information was enough to get Carolyn charged with bigamy, but was still a long way from homicide.

Further investigation revealed that Ray and Carolyn were only married for a year and a half and that Carolyn was the sole beneficiary of his estate and insurance policy.

Carolyn clearly had a motive to murder Ray.

With the mountain of circumstantial evidence stacked against her, many began to wonder why the bigamist had not been charged with murder. Many people have been charged and convicted with less evidence. What made the woman who became known as Carolyn Krizan-Wilson so special?

It turns out that in the years after Ray's murder, Carolyn inserted herself nicely into the local law enforcement establishment.

Two of Carolyn's sons went on to become officers with the Houston Police Department, and somehow Carolyn was able to land job as a civilian employee with the same department. No doubt Carolyn's connections with the police department were a mark in her favor, but they ultimately did not stop Harris County prosecutors from charging her with murder in 2008.

The charges were big news in the Houston area, and the ensuing court proceedings proved to only add to what was becoming a tabloid television type atmosphere surrounding the case.

Carolyn's attorneys argued that too much time had passed and there was no solid forensic evidence to tie their client to the crime, so the charges should be dropped. In a surprise move to many Houstonians, Judge Kevin Fine agreed and threw the case out of court, but Harris Count prosecutors proved relentless and appealed the decision. A Texas appellate court reinstated the charges in 2012, and word of a plea bargain began to surface shortly thereafter.

In 2013, Carolyn Krizan-Wilson was a shell of her former self. Frail and suffering from Alzheimer's disease at the age of seventy-one, prosecutors came to a deal with Krizan-Wilson's attorneys. Krizan-Wilson agreed to plead guilty to Roy's murder in return for a six-month jail sentence and probation for ten years.

Many thought that Krizan-Wilson should have spent the rest of her days in prison, but prosecutors were quick to point out that in the world we live in today that is obsessed with physical evidence, a hung jury or acquittal was a real possibility. Although some of Ray McCaleb's family did not share that sentiment, others were just glad to see Krizan-Wilson finally admit her guilt.

"She is willingly admitting that she murdered him and that's something we've known all these years," said Ray McCaleb's daughter Pam Nalley. "I think that means more to me than anything."

CHAPTER 11:
Robert Zarinsky – A Serial Killer Nabbed by DNA

There are some people among us who should never walk the streets free. These men, and sometimes women, are career criminals who do untold amounts of damage to society for sometimes long periods of time before they are usually sent to prison, only to be released one day so that they can return to the streets and prey on more victims. For every crime that these predators get caught committing, there are several more that they get away with, often including murder.

Robert Zarinsky was one such career criminal and predator. When he was not incarcerated in a prison, juvenile hall, or a mental hospital, he was on the streets victimizing the people of New Jersey. Eventually, Zarinsky was convicted of murder, but the parole system and sentencing guidelines meant that he could conceivably be released one day to prey on more innocent people. If Zarinsky could prove to a parole board that he was either reformed or no longer a threat to society, then he could be released.

Thanks to modern science, Zarinsky's DNA profile made sure that he would never hurt anyone again.

A Predator from the Beginning

Robert Zarinsky was born in 1940 to a middle class New Jersey family, although the family's income level was about the only thing that was "middle American" about the extremely dysfunctional family.

Robert showed signs of extreme violence and cruelty at a young age that are often the hallmarks of a future serial killer. He was known to torture animals and often beat his sister Judith, to which their mother, Veronica, told her son, "Don't hit her in the face."

Yes, the matriarch of the Zarinsky household doted on and enabled little Robert, which led the future serial killer to commit innumerable anti-social acts. He was never punished for anything he did and was even allowed to victimize his own father. According to those close to the Zarinsky family, Robert routinely dished out physical beatings to the father, Julius, and often took his earnings from the family store that he owned.

Zarinksy clearly received no direction in his childhood, which no doubt contributed to his criminal behavior, but there seemed to be something deeper in the man that set him apart from the average misguided individual.

Robert Zarinsky enjoyed being cruel.

As Zarinsky became a teenager, he learned new ways to inflict pain and misery on others. He gathered together a number of like-minded losers and formed a gang he called the Panthers. The Panthers employed Nazi imagery, even though Zarinsky's father was Jewish, and enjoyed terrorizing the residents around Linden, New Jersey, with acts of arson and vandalism. Zarinsky's reign of terror culminated at the age of twenty-two when he and his friends burned down five lumber yards and desecrated hundreds of tombstones in a Jewish cemetery. Robert claimed insanity and spent some time in a mental hospital.

Zarinsky was not cured; in fact, after Robert was released from the mental hospital he traveled around New Jersey, leaving a trail of bodies in his wake.

A Life of Murder and a Life in Prison

While most of the people in the United States were adjusting to the great social changes of the 1960s, Robert Zarinsky was apparently killing women throughout the state of New Jersey. The change in culture from the somewhat rigid rule structure of the 1950s to the permissive attitudes of the 1960s seemed to be the perfect backdrop for Zarinsky's murderous obsession with girls and young women. Unfortunately, the science needed to catch Zarinsky and other serial killers like him was still a few decades away. DNA profiling would not become commonplace in police investigations until the 1990s, and extensive use of close circuit television cameras was also a couple of decades in the future.

But the Robert Zarinksy case proves that with some patience, modern science has the ability to help identify and capture serial killers.

Although Zarinksy had been convicted of a number of serious felonies before the late 1960s, murder was not yet a crime on his resume of destruction.

In the summer of 1969, seventeen-year-old Rosemary Calandriello was a girl who was trying to find herself in the ever-changing world of the '60s. Calandriello was known to be a good girl, but like most kids her age, she wanted to fit in. Many of Calandriello's friends liked to drink some beer and smoke marijuana, although finding party favors could sometimes be a problem for the broke, underage high school kids.

Enter Robert Zarinksy.

Like a true predator, Zarinsky was known to show up at the parties of people ten years or more younger than him. As a criminal, Zarinsky usually had money, drugs, and a car. He was like the criminal pied piper of New Jersey, which turned out to be fatal for Rosemary Calandriello and a number of other girls and young women.

August 25, 1969, was the last night anyone saw Rosemary Calandrillo, as she seemingly disappeared into thin air, but she was last seen with Robert Zarinsky.

"We had four eyewitnesses who put the girl in his car," said district attorney John Mullaney. "Then we found the car, and the handles on the doors and the windows were missing."

Despite the eyewitnesses' testimonies and the suspicious circumstances of Zarinsky's lost and found car, prosecutors were slow to charge Zarinsky due to a lack of physical evidence and, most importantly, the absence of Calandriello's body.

Despite the lack of a body and very little physical evidence, Mullaney went ahead with the prosecution, and in 1975 Zarinsky earned the dubious distinction of being the first person convicted of murder in the state of New Jersey without a body. Zarinsky appealed the conviction and lost, but by the late 1980s, perhaps believing that he could obtain parole if he "came clean," Zarinsky admitted to murdering Calandriello. In typical sociopathic fashion, he mitigated his responsibility by stating that the murder was accidental. He also vacillated when asked where he disposed of her body: in one interview he said he buried her body in the hills of northwest New Jersey, while in another he claimed to have dumped Calandrillo's corpse in the Atlantic Ocean.

Although the possibility of parole was conceivable for Zarinsky, the time he spent in prison for Rosemary Calandriello's murder gave science and investigators time to catch up with the serial killer's other crimes.

Science Identifies a Serial Killer

The extent of the damage that Robert Zarinksy did to society was not known until fairly recently when scientific advances finally caught up the killer, but the first inkling that he may be a serial killer was revealed because of all things, a family dispute.

While Zarinksy was leading his Panthers gang destroying cemeteries and burning down lumber yards, he also took part in his first homicide. In 1958, when Zarinksy was eighteen, he and his cousin Theodore Schiffer were burglarizing a Pontiac car dealer in Rahway, New Jersey, when they were caught by a police officer.

The cop was a veteran named Charles Bernoskie who happened to see two young men lurking around the parking lot of the Pontiac dealer while he was on patrol. It was a totally random meeting.

Unfortunately for Bernoskie, the random encounter left him dead on the side of the road.

According to witness testimony taken years after the crime, Bernoskie surprised the two miscreants who then attempted to run. In an era long before "police brutality" was a common phrase, Bernoskie then apparently shot at and hit both fleeing suspects, who then returned fire, killing the officer.

"He pissed me off," said Zarinsky according to his sister, Judith Sapsa. "That's why I shot him."

Already seasoned criminals and therefore well aware of what could happen to them if they went to an emergency room, Zarinsky and Schiffer stumbled, bleeding, to Zarinsky's sister Judith Sapsa, who lived nearby. Luckily for the two men, no vital organs were hit, and after Judith and Veronica Zarinsky stitched the two up, they were ready to continue preying on the citizens of New Jersey.

But the murder of Charles Bernoskie was the first time that science caught up with one of Robert Zarinsky's crimes.

In 1999, a fingerprint taken from the crime scene was matched to Schiffer in the Automated Fingerprint Identification System (AFIS). The AFIS database works in much the same way as the CODIS database and essentially served as a template for it; all persons who are fingerprinted for a crime have their prints entered into the AFIS database, which is then used to solve cold cases among other things. It turns out that Schiffer was able to avoid arrest for all of those years, and Zarinsky, perhaps being the more sophisticated criminal, left no fingerprints at the scene. In a strange twist to the crime and an example of the bizarre dynamics of the dysfunctional Zarinsky family, Judith Sapsa implicated her brother as the shooter.

It seems that loyalty in the Zarinsky family only went as far as far as money would take it.

While Robert was serving his sentence for the murder of Rosemary Calandriello, he was able to amass a small fortune through some good investments. Apparently Judith had access to the mutual fund, and as her brother sat in prison, she embezzled a good chunk of it. Once Zarinsky learned of his sister's deception, he turned her in and she was promptly arrested for embezzling. She then saw her chance to get even when Schiffer was arrested for Bernoskie's murder.

The trial of both men turned out to be a lot of finger pointing with very little physical evidence. Schiffer ended up serving only three years for burglary and in 2001 Zarinsky was acquitted of murder. The jury cited the unreliable testimony of Sapsa and Schiffer as one of their primary reasons along with a lack of physical evidence.

But as DNA testing became more sophisticated and the CODIS database became more complete in the 2000s, the totality of Robert Zarinsky's murder spree was bound to surface with the light of day.

Although Zarinsky entered the prison system long before DNA profiling or the CODIS database existed, he, like all long-serving inmates in American prisons, was obliged to give a DNA sample in the 2000s. In the months just before he died in 2008 and in the years since, Zarinsky has been definitively identified through DNA matching as the killer of two girls and considered the likely suspect of at least four others.

After the murder of Charles Bernoskie, Zarinsky appears to have gone into a "cool down" period. Although it appears that Zarinsky did not plan to murder Bernoskie, the act seems to have kindled a dark, murderous desire that was dormant in him.

In 1965, Zarinsky acted on that dark impulse when he savagely raped and beat to death eighteen-year-old Mary Agnes Klinsky near Holmdel, New Jersey. After he was done with the young woman, he tossed her on the side of the road like trash, probably because he believed there was no way he could ever be linked to her.

In 2016, nearly eight years after his death, DNA conclusively linked Zarinsky to Klinsky's murder.

Zarinsky's next known murder took place when he abducted, raped, and murdered thirteen-year-old Jane Durrua on November 4, 1968. Apparently, Jane decided to take a short cut home through a field when she was swooped upon by Zarinksy. Her naked body was found the next day in the field.

Semen stains were taken from Durrua's clothing, but a mix-up in DNA samples originally led to the arrest of another man. After the problem was discovered and rectified, the sample was then matched to Zarinsky, which led to an indictment on March 11, 2008.

Zarinsky died while awaiting trial.

Even though Zarinsky is now dead, his DNA profile may still link him to a host of other murders. Seventeen-year-old Linda Balabanow was found raped and murdered in 1969, after she disappeared on her way to work in Union County, New Jersey. Then there was the case of fourteen-year-old Doreen Carlucci and her friend, fifteen-year-old Joanne Delardo, who were discovered together dead, naked in a field in 1974. The two girls had been raped, beaten, and strangled with an electrical cord. There was also nineteen-year-old Ann Logan, who was also found raped and beaten to death.

The magnitude of Zarinsky's crimes may never be fully known. Although it may be little comfort to the families of Zarinsky's victims, he spent the last years of his life in fear and pain. In 1999, once his initial case became public and it was announced that he was suspected in the murders of other girls and women in New Jersey, he was transferred from general population at the South Woods state prison to the protected custody block.

It seems that the man who could kill girls and women so easily was no match for the hardened convicts in the New Jersey prison system.

Finally, on November 28, 2008, after suffering from the painful effects of pulmonary fibrosis for some time, Robert Zarinsky died uneventfully in prison.

Although the psychopath took many unanswered questions with him to the grave, DNA profiling and the CODIS database helped prove that he was in fact a serial killer. The finding also helped give closure to some his victims' families.

"We knew he was a serial killer, but there was precious little to prove it," said John Mullaney.

Eventually, the science caught up and was able to uncover Zarinsky's evil deeds.

CHAPTER 12:
The Murder of Patricia Beard

In the United States, the most vulnerable of its citizens are not only protected by the government, but also given assistance. Mentally and physically disabled individuals are often housed in "group homes" where mental health professionals can look after them, and at the same time the residents are encouraged to take jobs in the community in order to realize their full potential. These group homes are safe havens for people with disabilities, as they offer places where the disabled can learn real-world skills as well as live in safety from the often cruel outside world.

Unfortunately for thirty-two-year-old Patricia Beard, a Denver group home could not protect her from the cruel clutches of a killer in 1981.

Patricia Beard was mentally disabled, but also what health care professionals would term a "high-functioning" individual who could work and interact in the larger community. The Denver group home where she lived was one that was there to help its residents with their medications, jobs, and other daily functions, but it was also a home that stressed independence and therefore gave the residents a certain amount of freedom.

Since Patricia Beard was a high functioning resident, staff members of the group home thought nothing when they did not see her for a couple of days. It was a group home, not a jail or halfway house, and its residents could come and go as they pleased. After a couple of more days, Patricia's friends and family started to worry when she did not answer her phone, so one of them went to her apartment and made a grisly discovery.

Patricia Beard was found dead in her room on March 27, 1981.

An investigation of the room by Denver homicide investigators revealed that Beard was strangled to death, and the fact that she was half-naked led them to believe that she was also raped. Vaginal swabs were later taken that confirmed that Patricia was raped before she was killed.

The investigation then turned to creating a list of suspects, but the police were soon discouraged as they met several dead-ends.

Staff at the group home reported seeing no strangers come to the home, and all residents and workers at the home were quickly cleared.

After searching the exterior of the group home, officers determined that the killer crawled into Beard's first floor apartment through a window. Homicide detectives then believed that the killer was a stranger, but probably someone with a record for burglary, sexual assault, or both. Police began their investigation by searching through all their records of burglars and sex offenders whose methods of operations matched the Beard murder. They were quickly let down when no credible matches were made.

Unfortunately, no fingerprints of the killer were lifted from the crime scene, but samples of semen were taken from Beard's vagina and mouth. The biological evidence was stored in an evidence locker where it sat for twenty years.

The Denver Cold Case Unit

The term "cold case" has become such a ubiquitous term in the modern lexicon that few today do not know what it means. Both fictional and documentary television shows that focus on police departments using forensics to capture killers in cases that took place years prior and are therefore considered "cold" are popular fare. Many of these shows depict the work as glamorous, but the reality is that is often tedious, time consuming, and just plain difficult. As depicted on some of these shows, over the last fifteen years, as the science of DNA profiling has progressed with the CODIS system, many police departments have created cold case units to solve murders like Patricia Beard's.

The Denver Cold Case Unit has proved to be one of the best in the world.

The Denver Police Department's cold case unit investigates both unsolved rapes and murders. The result is that the unit has solved more cold cases than any other similar unit in the world!

With such an elite unit working on Patricia Beard's murder, it was only a matter of time until her killer was captured. But first the unit had to get the case, which almost did not happen.

After Patricia Beard's apartment was processed, all of the items relevant to the case, such as the rape kit, were cataloged and then stored in the evidence locker at the Denver Police Department. There the evidence sat for thirteen years until most of it, with the exception of vaginal swabs, was destroyed to make room for evidence from other cases.

1994 would prove to be an important year in the Patricia Beard case, not just because potential DNA evidence was saved, but also because that was the year that the CODIS database went online.

In 2005, the Denver police department's crime lab and the Denver District Attorney's Office were selected to take part in a national study that investigated the impact of DNA profiling and the CODIS database on cold cases.

With that, the Denver Cold Case Unit was born.

116

As the unit moved through the remainder of the 2000s and into the 2010s solving cold cases, a detective re-discovered the rape kit from the Patricia Beard murder. Officers entered the evidence into the CODIS system, and in 2013 a match came back for a man named Hector Bencoma-Hinojos.

Bencoma-Hinojos was doing time in a federal prison in Pennsylvania, which therefore required him to give a sample of his DNA profile to the CODIS database. Although the DNA match meant that Bencoma-Hinojos had been sexually intimate with Beard, it did not necessarily mean that he killed or even raped her.

The Denver Cold Case Unit would have to conduct a more thorough investigation of their suspect.

A background check of Bencoma-Hinojos revealed that he was a known criminal and thief who had up until that point avoided doing any major prison time. He was also known to be extremely violent. His wife said that he would routinely threaten and beat her for the slightest indiscretions, and he often carried a knife.

Denver police then traveled to Pennsylvania to interview their captive suspect and, as it turns out, Bencoma-Hinojos' own words proved to be the last nails in his legal coffin.

Bencoma-Hinojos admitted to the authorities that he lived in Denver for several years beginning around 1977 and that he was probably living in the city in 1981, although he was evasive with his answers. The Cold Case Unit detectives then asked Bencoma-Hinojos if he knew Beard, which he answered in the negative. The police then gave their subject one last chance at a way out by showing him a picture of Beard, who was black, and asking him if it were possible that he had sex with the woman. Bencoma-Hinojos vehemently denied ever having sex with Beard and added that he had never had sex with a black woman.

The police caught Bencoma-Hinojos in a lie that the man's own DNA sample could verify!

In 2015, at the age of fifty-five, Hector Bencoma-Hinojos was sentenced to forty eight years in Colorado's Department of Corrections, which will more than likely amount to a life sentence for the middle aged murderer.

Bencoma-Hinojos' conviction proved to be a milestone as it was the 100th case solved by the Denver Police Department's Cold Case Unit.

Conclusion

All twelve of the cases examined in this book are amazing and mysterious in their own unique ways. Advances in DNA profiling have helped solve the mysteries of some of these cold case murders, while new eyewitness testimony has contributed to another being solved. In the future, DNA evidence may even identify more victims of the notorious serial killer Robert Zarinsky.

With that said, some mysteries remain.

The disappearance of the Palmer brothers in the vast wilderness of Alaska is a case that neither DNA nor eye-witness testimony appears likely to solve. Unfortunately for the Palmer family, it is as if the Alaskan mountains just swallowed Michael and Chucky whole along with any explanation of what happened.

Eye-witness testimony may help solve the enigmatic coincidence of the Mary Morris murders, but until that time people are left to wonder if the cases were connected or just another bizarre coincidence.

Finally, some cases, such as the Brighton Trunk Murders, defy any logical explanation and serve as proof that anything is possible and as far as man has advanced scientifically speaking, some things are just out of the realm of science.

Yes, the world is an amazing and mysterious place and as this book proves, sometimes crime plays a role in the mysteries of the world.

More books by Jack Rosewood

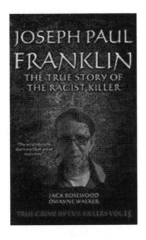

Among the annals of American serial killers, few were as complex and prolific as Joseph Paul Franklin. At a gangly 5'11, Franklin hardly looked imposing, but once he put a rifle in his hands and an interracial couple in his cross hairs, Joseph Paul Franklin was as deadly as any serial killer. In this true crime story you will learn about how one man turned his hatred into a vocation of murder, which eventually left over twenty people dead across America. Truly, Franklin's story is not only that of a true crime serial killer, but also one of racism in America as he chose Jews, blacks, and especially interracial couples as his victims.

Joseph Paul Franklin's story is unique among serial killers biographies because he gained no sexual satisfaction from his murders and there is no indication that he was ever compelled to kill. But make no mistake about it, by all definitions; Joseph Paul Franklin was a serial killer. In fact, the FBI stated that Franklin was the first known racially motivated serial killer in the United States: he planned to kill as many of his perceived enemies as possible in order to start an epic race war across the country. An examination of Franklin's life will reveal how he became a racially motivated serial killer and the steps he took to carry out his one man war against the world.

Open the pages of this e-book to read a disturbing story of true crime murder in America's heartland. You will be disturbed and perplexed at Franklin's murderous campaign as he made himself a one man death squad, eliminating as many of his political enemies that he could. But you will also be captivated with Franklin's shrewdness and cunning as he avoided the authorities for years while he carried out his diabolical plot!

When Chris Bryson was discovered nude and severely beaten stumbling down Charlotte Street in Kansas City in 1988, Police had no idea they were about to discover the den of one of the most sadistic American serial killers in recent history. This is the true historical story of Robert Berdella, nicknamed by the media the Kansas City Butcher, who from between 1984 and 1988 brutally raped, tortured and ultimately dismembered 6 young male prostitutes in his unassuming home on a quiet street in Kansas City.

Based on the actual 720 page detailed confession provided by Berdella to investigators, it represents one of the most gruesome true crime stories of all time and is unique in the fact that it details each grizzly murder as told by the killer himself. From how he captured each man, to the terrifying methods he used in his torture chamber, to ultimately how he disposed of their corpses - rarely has there ever been a case where a convicted serial killer confessed to police in his own words his crimes in such disturbing detail.

Horrific, shocking and rarely equaled in the realms of sadistic torture – Berdella was a sexually driven lust killer and one of the most sadistic sex criminals ever captured. Not for the faint of heart, this is the tale of Robert "Bob" Berdella, the worst serial killer in Kansas City History and for those that are fans of historical serial killers, is a true must read.

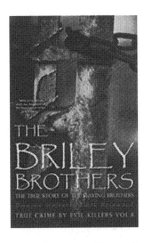

Richmond, Virginia: On the morning of October 19, 1979, parolee James Briley stood before a judge and vowed to quit the criminal life. That same day, James met with brothers Linwood, Anthony, and 16-year-old neighbor Duncan Meekins. What they planned—and carried out—would make them American serial-killer legends, and reveal to police investigators a 7-month rampage of rape, robbery, and murder exceeding in brutality already documented cases of psychopaths, sociopaths, and sex criminals.

As reported in this book, the Briley gang were responsible for the killing of 11 people (among these, a 5-year-old boy and his pregnant mother), but possibly as many as 20. Unlike most criminals, however, the Briley gang's break-ins and robberies were purely incidental—mere excuses for rape and vicious thrill-kills. When authorities (aided by plea-bargaining Duncan Meekins) discovered the whole truth, even their tough skins crawled. Nothing in Virginian history approached the depravities, many of which were committed within miles of the Briley home, where single father James Sr. padlocked himself into his bedroom every night.

But this true crime story did not end with the arrests and murder convictions of the Briley gang. Linwood, younger brother James, and 6 other Mecklenburg death-row inmates, hatched an incredible plan of trickery and manipulation—and escaped from the "state-of-the-art" facility on May 31, 1984. The biggest death-row break-out in American history.

During fifty one days in early 1993 one of the most tragic events in American crime history unfolded on the plains outside Waco, Texas. An obscure and heavily armed religious sect called the Branch Davidians was barricaded inside their commune and outside were hundreds of law enforcement angry because the former had killed four ATF agents in a botched raid. Open the pages of this book and go on an engaging and captivating ride to examine one of the most important true crime stories in recent decades. Read the shocking true story of how a man the government considered a psychopath, but whose followers believed to be a prophet, led a breakaway sect of the Seventh Day Adventist Church into infamy.

You will follow the meteoric rise of the Branch Davidians' charismatic leader, David Koresh, as he went from an awkward kid in remedial classes to one of the most infamous cult leaders in world history. But the story of the Waco Siege begins long before the events of 1993. At the core of the conflict between the Branch Davidians and the United States government were ideas and interpretations of religious freedom and gun ownership, which as will be revealed in the pages of this book, a considerable philosophical gulf existed between the two sides. David Koresh and the Branch Davidians carried on a long tradition in American and Texas history of religious dissent, but in 1993 that dissent turned tragically violent.

You will find that beyond the standard media portrayals of the Waco Siege was an event comprised of complex human characters on both sides of the firing line and that perhaps the most tragic aspect of the event was that the extreme bloodshed could have been avoided.

The pages of this book will make you angry, sad, and bewildered; but no matter the emotions evoke, you will be truly moved by the events of the Waco Siege.

GET THESE BOOKS FOR FREE

Go to www.jackrosewood.com

and get these E-Books for free!

A Note From The Author

Hello, this is Jack Rosewood. Thank you for reading this book. I hope you enjoyed the read. If you did, I'd appreciate if you would take a few moments to post a review on Amazon.

I would also love if you'd sign up to my newsletter to receive updates on new releases, promotions and a FREE copy of my Herbert Mullin E-Book, www.JackRosewood.com

Thanks again for reading this book, make sure to follow me on Facebook.

Best Regards

Jack Rosewood

95212415R00080